SUNSHINE
IS
EVERYWHERE

SUNSHINE
IS
EVERYWHERE

ONE MOMENT AT A TIME

Pradeep Malhotra

WANDERINGS, MUSINGS, REFLECTIONS

Notion Press

Old No. 38, New No. 6
McNichols Road, Chetpet
Chennai - 600 031

First Published by Notion Press 2017

ISBN 978-1-946515-32-2

This book is dedicated to

Sri Aurobindo and The Mother

and to my parents,

whose presence though unseen,

is always deeply felt.

Contents

HONEYBEES IN SEARCH OF GOLD

CATCH ME IF YOU CAN

Dr. Karan Singh
MEMBER OF PARLIAMENT
(RAJYA SABHA)

3, NYAYA MARG
CHANAKYAPURI
NEW DELHi - 110 021

FOREWORD

In all the darkness that seems to surround us due to social turmoil, economic stress and political conflict, it is tremendously important to maintain a balanced and positive view of life. Too many people these days tend to fall into negative and depressive states which only further exacerbate the situation. I am glad that Pradeep Malhotra has dedicated his musings to Sunshine. A nature lover, a resident of the hills and an avid reader, he spends his time between Delhi and his home in Bhimtal in the Kumaon Himalayas around which he wanders, explores and indulges in extensive reflection.

The mountains are indeed the best place for creativity and introspection, which is why down to this day most of our ashrams and spiritual centres are located there. Indeed it is the Himalayas that have given us the Vedas, the Upanishads and other great texts. The Kumaon hills are particularly attractive, and I have had many occasions to visit them. Indeed I have even built myself a 'Sanyas Kutia' in a village beyond Ranikhet, although I hardly ever visit it and have still not donned the ochre robes !

Pradeep has a facile pen, and in his journal touches upon a range of issues that the reader will find of interest. They range from environmental concerns, social interactions and most important of all the spiritual quest. Many of his pieces contain a wealth of good sense and even inspiration. I have pleasure in commending the book to nature lovers wherever they may be.

Karan Singh
Sept. 22, 2016

Tel. : 2611-1744, 2611-5291 Fax : 2687-3171
E-mail : karansingh@karansingh.com

Preface

These reflections are part of an on-going personal journey—wanderings and musings on the many transitions encountered on the way. They are brief pauses in a journey where we observe ourselves and the events around us. In silence, we reflect on the direction of these movements. It is perhaps only when we slow down that thoughts deep within us have a chance to surface. Over the years, Sunday morning walks at the Sunlit Path, Sri Aurobindo Ashram, New Delhi, have given the opportunity to pause and ponder, with sunshine pouring into my being. To Sri Aurobindo Ashram and its environs, I express my deep gratitude.

We always forget that with all things taken care of, we should just be. All things are being taken care of, nothing is missing. Today, we sense an evolutionary acceleration and discern a veiled intervention taking us in an unknown direction, perhaps towards a newer consciousness and way of being. In our intuitive moments, we perceive an ineffable, mysterious presence and witness a smile that dances with all that surrounds us. We have only to be present in these moments. My long stays at 'Dharini,' Bhimtal, in the Kumaon Himalayas, in the midst of nature and in rural surroundings, with the heady smell of shrubs and wood smoke and the comforting sounds and bustle of birds, cows, cats and children, have sensitised me to this aspect and helped me bring it to your attention.

Over the years, our small 'Friday readings' group of friends has been a source of immense support. We have been meeting each month, reading from Sri Aurobindo and The Mother's writings, sharing notes on life and events on the way. Our individual aspirations and journeys, the social crisis of our times, questions posed by nature and environment and the quest for the spiritual, both at the individual and collective levels, have spurred many a discussion. Today, we greatly miss the presence of Mrs Sima Sharma, editor at the India International Centre, New Delhi, who was a source of great encouragement and spiritual and intellectual stimulation.

I acknowledge a debt of gratitude to my friend Sukanya Bose, who kindly went through this manuscript and offered her valuable suggestions, and to Ann Vinod and her team at Notion Press, for their creative inputs and efforts to make this book possible.

I am especially grateful to my family who have always been a source of great support and who, over the years, gave me the freedom, space and sanctuary to just be.

– Pradeep Malhotra

auroharmony7@gmail.com

# SUNSHINE EVERYWHERE

One can Never Tell...

Things happen when they are destined to. Each thing carries within it the seeds of its destiny, hidden from view. Similarly, these notebooks lay in a cupboard awaiting their hour of use. Everything is now falling into place, every thing. Even our errors have some deep meaning. They are the means to take us to a better place, provide us a better resolution and some greater harmony.

Photo: Pradeep Malhotra

The sun is shimmering through the mist. I wonder what it foretells for the day. The dew glistens on the grass. I can hear the sound of a *jharoo* cleaning a room and of wheat grains being sifted. My friend, the cat, makes her presence felt. Where are her offspring, I wonder? She has made this *diwan* bed her favourite spot for feeding her kittens.

Each day, my thoughts cross boundaries and I ponder, crisscrossing across time and life's experiences, the many joys and sorrows that have brought me to where I am. The mist of the hills and the smell of the hill plants, shrubs and wood smoke draw me back time and again; perhaps, the mist and smoke have got into my blood.

The day grows warmer, suggesting a respite from the rain, but one can never tell. That is the enduring charm and mystery of the hills, that one can never tell.

Where is this Journey Taking Me?

I reach the Kumaon hills early in the morning as the sun rises through the mist. I will return to Delhi only some weeks later. Life seems to be a series of comings and goings. Where exactly are we going to or coming from? We are not quite sure. It seems a long, continuing, endless journey, never quite arriving anywhere. Can I ever say that I have truly arrived? Before I can say that, I start preparations for the next journey. Even as I reach my destination and start unpacking, my mind is preoccupied by arrangements for the return journey.

Why can't we fully be where we are? Right now, I am at this writing table and I need to be fully here. I need to be where I am. Just be there. I need to watch my mind and its movements. The mind needs something to hold on to, to chew on, from moment to moment. It could be anything, the not-so-satisfactory present or the uncertain future. It could be an object of desire or longing. It could be a past hurt. It could be an anticipated joy or a projection into the future. The mind has a great ability to chew on anything it gets. It is a great illusionist, a great projectionist. It can send life uphill or downhill.

All journeys start in the mind; they end there too. Let each part of our ever-continuing journey be appreciated from moment to moment, even as the landscape changes from minute to minute, never remaining the same. We need fresh eyes at each moment to enjoy the scenery if we are to be one with a divine consciousness, a streaming consciousness, and conscious of itself from moment to moment, enjoying its creation afresh at each moment and renewing itself constantly.

Perhaps, these are what journeys are about—each journey a drawing of experiences along the way. With each experience, we recharge ourselves. We want more and more, till one day we are saturated. We start to see all experiences as one and the same. It could be this way or that, high or low, hot or cold. All experiences make up a consciousness running through time, ever widening, ever evolving, taking all things that come its way, encompassing all in its light, embracing all, loving all, excluding and rejecting nothing.

We sense this light of a new consciousness filling every crevice in creation, fulfilling an eternal promise the Divine has made—the promise to transform all things in its image, to transform all journeys into a single sublime one.

Going High, Going Solo

The sun is out, bright and inviting. A bumble bee ventures into the veranda and hovers around while I have my morning tea. A beautiful and awesome creature to behold. Let me take a picture…but it flies away the moment my camera is poised. Some of us are born camera-shy!

Now, for some breakfast…a traditional one of *aloo paratha*, buffalo milk, curd and chilly pickle—I could ask for nothing more!

Photo: Pradeep Malhotra

I finish reading a book that I greatly enjoy—Roald Dahl's escapades during World War II with vintage aircraft for company. They take me back in time to happy memories of my very first job with a small outfit that undertook agricultural crop-spray operations in the border areas of Punjab and Rajasthan with tiny, low-flying, crop-hugging aircraft and bubbletop helicopters. Could anything have been more exciting when one is barely out of college? At a distance above the valley, a lone eagle circles the sky, heightening this memory.

The solitary chatter of a jungle babbler punctures the air. Strange…where are the rest? The *saat bhai* or jungle babblers are always together. And then, suddenly, in answer to my question, comes the raucous babble of the rest of its clan. The trees and shrubs surrounding our home 'Dharini' give these birds good cover. I realise that they too are an integral part of a co-evolution that surrounds us all.

The children of the caretaker farm-keepers are on holiday. It is Children's Day, followed by Muharram and other holidays. Leelu, the eldest, is repairing the edges of my blanket, which have been nibbled by a marauding mouse with a taste for the finer things in life. I plan to take on a couple of cane chairs and give them a dab of spirit polish. This place needs a coat of paint; there are too many damp spots in an assorted jumble of shapes and sizes after the rains. I speak to Leelu; she seems to understand just what needs be done. Today, Hema, our farm-keeper and caretaker's wife, and the neighbouring women will be collecting fodder for the cows from the neighbouring Pande Gaon and will be back only by late evening.

I am lucky to be leading this rural life so often. I am lucky in many ways, but the realisation is slow to come. Perhaps, I need to realign myself to some truths. But what is the truth? Perhaps, all life, all experience, has its own truth; it hides many things too. There are many shades to truth, but we see only what we can. All things move towards a larger truth, towards a greater whole, a greater completion, but are never fully complete. Perhaps, we are beings in progress, transitional beings on our way to an eternal destiny. Yet, this knowledge is slow to come; at times, we feel stuck, trapped.

Perhaps, these traps create an opening too, as we go deep within, as we silence our inner selves in the face of the clamour of life and living. At the heart of all things is an abiding peace. Listen closely; even in the face of clash and clamour, there are the separating moments of silence and peace. All things have meaning only in the backdrop of, on a canvas of, silence. May we be rooted in, enveloped in, silence. May our flight be like that of the golden eagle as it hovers silently, watching all things so majestically, even as it goes higher and higher, flying solo!

Half Clear, Half Full of Thunder

The sun is out, bright and shining—a nice contrast to yesterday's mist and rain in our valley. The mother cat and the kittens run playfully all over…and now suddenly, there is a lull.

Things green are in wild profusion, the flowers are colourful and bright with yesterday's rain drops still glistening. The kittens hovering near my table wonder if breakfast is forthcoming as young Kabbu brings out a cup and plates from the kitchen. I worry for Kabbu; she has dropped out from school, she likes to do everything but study. Is it for me to worry? Perhaps some other power sees all, takes care of all.

I hear shrill bird calls. I wonder where they are hidden. Then, a distant call of a partridge. A bee buzzes near the flower hedge. My clothes are drying on the rope hanging between trees. Tin roofs shine in the distance. A butterfly flits by. A crow caws raucously. Flies congregate in droves near the veranda.

A hearty breakfast before the day's activities begin at our little farm home and vegetable patch. This is for now; just a bit later, I shall need tea, coffee! But for the moment, I am content, at ease with myself and the world.

And then I hear this murmur—is it from outside or from my own heart? Who knows, who can tell? Some uncertainty holds the key. All things are in a state of becoming, all things are moving to another state; nothing is static, not even for a moment. In the blink of an eye, the scene has changed, and we struggle with memories! Our lives are in a state of perennial quandary—what next, what next? We have not lived this moment but are always thinking, 'what next'. Something is always missing; the heart misses a beat. My friends, the cats, are back. Have they had their fill or do they think another snack awaits them?

The day is ready for me, but am I ready for the day? I hear the moo of a cow and a blur of sounds from a distance—birds make their presence felt, there is the clatter of pots and pans being cleaned. I sense life moving on, regardless of what anyone thinks or feels. Suddenly, without notice or warning, dense clouds cover the sun; rain clouds are gathering again and I behold in wonder—half the sky is clear but the other half is full of thunder.

Half is clear, half is full of thunder!

I Bond with Ruskin

I look out of the window of my home in the Kumaon hills. I think of how I would like to write like my old friend Ruskin Bond, with a languid patience, about things one has seen or done, but words escape me. I am not as eloquent or effortless with words or with my pen. But perhaps I could try…and then, try again.

Ruskin can write on nature, on birds, on flowers, on hills, rivers and streams. He observes in minute detail happenings that might, to the superficial eye, seem so humdrum, so common place. His feelings and his writings merge ever so softly; he conjures a simpler time, a more leisurely pace. I readily slip back to my school days when I read his books; those days were quite some time ago. The country was still in the sunset ambience of the empire gone into retreat. My teachers, the last of the British stragglers, were heading home.

Photo: Pradeep Malhotra

The remnants of the Raj were strewn everywhere: old sprawling bungalows; sleepy yet efficient cantonments; army bands playing languid Scottish tunes; liveried bearers and cooks; rest houses with their barely stirring fans in far-off places; easy armchairs with long protruding footrests; first-class rail travel with unmatched privacy and comfort; *vindaloo curry*; bread pudding; *pilau*; railway cutlets; long summer holidays in cool, lush green hill stations; travel in style on ponies or on the occasional *dandi*. Those were the days of *chotta hazri* in the morning, the barber calling home on Sundays and grand, unforgettable Christmas parties. Tea planters entertained at exclusive clubs and embarked on leisurely home leave by P&O ships to London! *Chotta* pegs and *burra* pegs and *koi hais* to answer every call! Perhaps some remnants still linger…

I could go on and on. Yes, there was something endearing to that life that I do miss. I miss its leisure, its style, its comforts, its certitude—everything *pukka*! Privilege came as genteel leisure. But that time has now gone; those leisurely days are gone forever, replaced with I know not what. All things are now in a terrible hurry, at rocket speed, going where, no one knows. A mishmash of everything, a *khichree*! All the old colours, the old delectable flavours, are lost, in what seems like a blink.

Ruskin's writings, his memoirs, gently mourn the lonely, missing years of his childhood, of times gone past. They bridge cultures and timeframes and chronicle a period in transition. They yearn for this older, quieter pace of life. He now lives with his memories in splendid isolation, cut off from the rush and clamour of cities, in his mountain retreat. Yet, even while there, he remains connected, and how! Lesser mortals head off to the hills to experiment with the slow and easy every now and then, but something is not quite the same as it once used to be. The older, gentler, slower way of life is fading fast in front of our wondering eyes; a new paradigm is struggling to take its place, still very unsure of itself or of where it is headed. Perhaps, something else is evolving. It is a time for other voices to be heard, for other stories to be told.

As we reflect, as we ponder, can we not meld the best of the old to the evolving new in some happy synthesis or creative fusion? Can we not link our dreams with a living, pulsating rainbow where all things play their destined roles to perfection—man, flowers, birds, hills and mountain streams? Can we not have a place where man can proudly live off the sweat of his brow, a life of creativity, leisure and interdependence? Can we not have a place where his imagination takes him—with the birds, with the flowers, with the stars—where he can let gently flowing streams beguile him or the call of the jungle fowl take him on a wild goose chase? It would be a place where big or small, high or low loses all meaning, where all things are seen through a twinkling, tranquil calm, through a placid, equal gaze.

Hullabaloo in the Veranda

There is a hullabaloo in the veranda—the sparrows are at it. Are they making a home or running a discotheque? I've never heard so much noise, so much *hungama* in my life! Now, a wandering puppy and a neighbouring cow have joined this raucous melee.

Just yesterday, I took a nice, serene walk from the Kausani guesthouse through a forest path, stopping en route to photograph flowers, trees, signboards and some monkeys hell-bent on providing free entertainment near an upturned pine tree. Then, I see an enchanting sight—a *pahari* lady, colourfully and delicately dressed with a large red *bindi* on her forehead, a nose ring and bangles, walking slowly, gracefully down a winding pathway. She has a gentle smile on her lips.

I amble my way to the Anashakti Ashram, where Mahatma Gandhi stayed in 1929, a laidback place where time seems to have stood still. Only a small, motley group of students and tourists are milling around a bookstore. I get a spectacular view of the Himalayan peaks—the Trisul, Nandadevi and Panchchuli. I have a sudden realisation of how much of the old simplicity and slow pace of life we have lost, and yes, what a loss of grace it is.

I am lucky to catch a bus going straight to Bhowali, passing and stopping en route through many villages which have a familiar ring from my childhood spent here—Gwalkot; Patlibagad; Devasthal; Dharanaula; Khinapani;

Suyalbadi; Khairna, a favourite picnic spot along the Kosi river; Garampani; Ramgarh; Betalghat. These are sleepy hamlets and their names bring back memories and the desire for a slower, simpler life. But going back to a simpler life may be far more complicated than I imagine.

Can we ever go back into a past long gone? A new paradigm is evolving, but perhaps, we cannot see it yet. Its contours are for us to shape; we can join the spiritual to the ecological, the practical, the economic, and the day-to-day. We must link the divine with the ordinary, the everyday. Can anything that the Divine created be ordinary, commonplace?

We are integral parts of an evolution that is increasingly picking up speed. Our role is becoming clearer. We are co-evolvers on an eternal journey. May we go into the deepest silence of our minds and hearts and there discover what has been lying hidden, a vein of gold leading straight to the source, to the living, loving, forever-vibrating, pulsating, transcendent divine.

This hullabaloo too is divine.

Harela

Today heralds '*harela*,' an important event here in the Kumaon hills—the onset of the monsoon rains and the greening of the mountains. Agriculture-based communities in this region consider it auspicious, as it marks the beginning of the sowing season. I visit the *Harela Mela* at the Ram Lila fairgrounds with my friend, Bhuvan, on his much-travelled and hill-tested motorbike.

Photo: Pradeep Malhotra

The fairgrounds are full of slush from the rains, but the children and elders don't seem to mind at all and are making the most of the event. The stalls are makeshift tents of tarpaulin selling colourful and gaudy goods—plastic buckets and pans, crockery, children's clothes, women's sarees, toys, odds and ends. An interesting stall is being run by a cheerful young hill boy from a remote border district. He has woollen goods, jackets, mufflers and a mysterious range of herbs I have never encountered. I like him. He is a good salesman, friendly yet not too forcefully insistent.

Bhuvan tries out some *pahari* woollen jackets and sniffs at some herbs to gauge their efficacy and strength! The boy sets aside a few items for us to pick up later. The stall next door, run by his mother and sister, keeps some things not stocked by him; they are complementing their efforts and a quiet synergy prevails.

Near the merry-go-round and Ferris wheel, the fair's high point where every child seems to congregate, I bump into my friend Peter's wife, Rajni, and their daughter. Peter specialises in collecting and studying hill insects and butterflies. I have spent some interesting moments with him at his June Estate cottage, observing the pond and forest patch where leopards still visit. His father was from Sudetenland, Czechoslovakia, and had jumped ship during the Second World War and made the Kumaon hills his home. His side of the hill is cloaked with a dense growth of oak trees within which nestles a small butterfly sanctuary. He is happy to give visitors an introduction to butterflies and moths, of which he has one of the largest collections in India, and to speak on the ecology of the region.

Getting home, I walk through our damp vegetable patch and the land surrounding it. Where is the bougainvillea we planted last season? I can count a mere three or four plants, submerged in a wild profusion of wild *terai* grass and *kurri* or lantana, the scourge of the hills, that swamps even the barbed-wire fencing. I think we must work on each stretch of the boundary bit by bit, removing this parasite pest and introducing some local flowering shrubs and trees.

I read an interesting book, *The No 1 Ladies Detective Agency*. I admire its style and wit and the delicious use of local colour. The place names, flora and fauna reduce Gaborone to its essentials, its bare outlines, against which its protagonist stands out sharp, with a quirky simplicity. I enjoy the cut-out characters that gain shape and substance as the plot thickens. An interesting thought flits through the mind—perhaps someday, I too might write a novel!

My jeans caked with damp soil, my shoes soaked wet, my mood swings with the rain-darkened sky. Yes, the mood of *harela* has entered my being, energising my spirit. I am ready to dance to its tune.

My Mind Just Wanders... No Destination

The sun is out bright and early, a cow moos contentedly, bees buzz here and there—the world is at peace. A bird's shrill cry sounds. I spy a sunbird swinging on the branch of the bottlebrush tree. A dog barks lazily, without force or conviction.

I ring my friend Mike to inform him of roses and sunshine in these parts, to check to see if he would like to join in a repast. There is no answer; perhaps, he is catching up on sleep. I read a book, John Laing's *The Himalaya Club*. It is an old book, written around the time of the great Indian mutiny. With puckish humour and a storyteller's flair, the author brings to life the early years of the British Raj, sketching scandals and a farcical court martial and other sundry diversions in Kussowlie and Simlah!

And then, a random thought came to me early this morning: are chance and desire an instrument of evolution to take consciousness forward? With each desire, with each chance happening, perhaps even a thwarting of that desire, we move forward towards some higher resolution. We are where we are at this moment because of some higher reality, some juxtaposition of forces and circumstances far greater than our personal resolve or motivation. Perhaps, that is the best possible outcome under the circumstances. The world situation, each one's own situation is probably the best under the circumstances.

Then, more random thoughts come: what of that death I witnessed the other day, was that the best too? The death of a young father, the destruction of a beautiful family and its hopes—was that too for the best? And what of all those dreams and longings I once had? Where do they lie? Forgotten? Shattered? All those things I had so fondly imagined, hoped for—what of those? Do they lie forlorn in some dusty memory, lonely figures and ephemeral, gone with some gust of breeze? And then one day, a fine dust covers even those memories. The time spirit moves on unrelenting. It holds on to nothing, releasing all as it moves.

A gong sounds. Is it a school or a temple? An hour is over, a new one begins? Our self-created routines, do they mean anything? Are they a method to while away time, till the time to go comes? Can I abdicate time's demands? Who can tell? The sound of a temple conch rends the air. What does it say? Is it an invocation to some deity, a call to one's own soul? A blank silence follows. Does it need to be filled or do we become that silence? In silence, we witness the world and perhaps the call of our own hearts too.

A grazing pony calls out to its mate, a calf to its mother. Things are never still; there is always some movement. I hear a ladle against a cooking pot. Someone walks in. My heart wonders what to make of this moment. Am I happy … am I sad? I look on with a witness' gaze? How does it matter? How does anything matter? Can I just take each thing as it comes? I see children walk hand-in-hand across our garden path. They have no program, no agenda. My mind wanders, just wanders… no destination.

Pleasures of a Tangled Trip Through Kumaon Hills

It was an eventful day, a journey with many ups and downs. A decision not to take the well-trodden route came with a price.

We had travelled by car from Bhimtal to Jageshwar via Padampuri, with all the scenic interludes that the Uttarakhand hills in India so spectacularly provide. Local customs and ancient traditions are still alive here. We get a glimpse of these through the temples, traditional *aepan* paintings and the charming Kumaoni houses set among many green terraces. Each season brings its own magic. Spring brings its blue skies; fruit trees blossom and forests turn a flaming red with rhododendron flowers. Autumn comes with golden sunshine and hills dotted with cosmos flowers and wild cherry trees in bloom. Winter is crisp and clear with the sweet scent of mimosa filling the air.

Photo: Pradeep Malhotra

But on this trip—in peak summer, in June, before the rains had begun and when the sun-soaked hills were scorched dry—we decided to bypass Almora, to take a short cut. Before we realised, the road had disappeared altogether! We were on a rubble-strewn, potholed track leading endlessly to nowhere. En route, a forest fire nearly scorched us with red hot cinders falling into our moving car. We encountered heat, dust and smoke from road rollers on the move and coal tar being heated; fallen boulders and deep pits had to be negotiated and not a single '*chai*' shop or habitation was visible for us to ask for directions. Bypassing Almora had turned out to be no option at all—a nightmare! So, it was grudgingly back to Almora for us, and then onwards to Jageshwar, which lies at an elevation of 1,870 metres.

Jageshwar came as a pleasant surprise, with a cool breeze blowing. It is a beautiful narrow valley surrounded by a dense forest of magnificent, ancient deodar trees, 34 kilometres from Almora and the abode of twelve *jyotirlings*. The area has 124 temples and hundreds of statues believed to have been constructed from the seventh century, a period of deep cultural and religious fervour when there was great temple building activity under the Katyuri kings. For over a century, the area served as a transit point for spiritual seekers visiting the holy Mansarovar in the Tibetan plateau by foot, across the Himalayan mountains.

The walk to our lodge is a great experience, undertaken through a forest that has a cool, damp stream, gurgling and babbling intermittently. It takes us a while to negotiate the stretch as we breathlessly halt at every bend. We are tired after a long journey, my friend Mike more so, after the long drive and his present depleted health.

As we approach, we realise what a lovely place we have come to. En route, we encounter a young lady of foreign origin, sitting meditatively by the stream, no doubt captivated by the sound of the stream and the bird calls. We spy the Himalayan bulbul and the red-billed blue magpie as they move from tree to tree. The lilting sounds of a *pahari* song *'Bedu pako baramasa,'* coming from a distance, are captivating. Do I hear bagpipes too? Our lodge guide tells us there is a marriage in the neighbourhood. A lone bagpiper playing *pahari* tunes is a tradition. Bagpipe music was introduced among the common people of Garhwal and Kumaon by the retired army personnel of the British Garhwal Rifles.

Our arrival is greeted with a nice cup of tea accompanied by bread and *pakoras*. We indulge in yet another cup before we venture out to explore the neighbourhood. I spy a small temple, ancient and abandoned, hidden amongst the bramble. As I peer into the dark, I see a couple of idols and tell-tale signs that some wandering monk still uses it as his place of meditation. We have a choice: to soak in the spiritual energy of this area or go for a hike in the surrounding woods. We choose the latter.

This place is pure Corbett country. I can almost see a leopard along the stream or lurking up some terrace that is green with bush and trees, mostly oak, pine and fir, the scent of which wafts on the fresh breeze. The forests around Binsar and Jageshwar have a wide range of animals including barking deer, black bear, serow (the goat-like antelope), *sambhar* and a wide variety of birdlife including the chestnut-bellied rock thrush and rufus sibia. We wander, enchanted, through the forest fringes and a hidden meadow, imagining a glimpse in the rustling of leaves and among the many dark shadows.

As evening sets, it turns cold and we head back. A campfire is lit and a wafting pine smell brings back memories. We remember our old friend Shankar and our many escapades together over the years. Food and drinks are laid out alongside a crackling fire. Our lodge hosts, Ramesh and Pran, are young and helpful. The drinks make us heady. My friend manoeuvres his camera near the fire, taking pictures that surprise me. He shows an amazing dexterity. His years of travel with his camera have sensitised him. We are seeing each other after many years and have a lot of catching up to do.

We enjoy a nice dinner that is well-cooked, *pahari* style, with potatoes fried in mustard oil also thrown in. An early morning is planned for tomorrow. I have had my fill for the day, I think, as I head to bed. On my bedside is Jan Morris's *Pleasures of a Tangled Life*! How appropriate, I think. A tangled trip full of memories; could it have been better or otherwise?

Not a Kitten Care in the World

As I prepare to settle down to jotting notes in my diary, I find Sonu, the kitten, curled up on my tiny writing-cum-dining table, not the least concerned that I too might have need of it. It is siesta time for her, and that is that. It is a nice, clear day that is gradually warming up, although in the covered veranda, it feels cool, cold too. I read Amit Chaudhary's *Calcutta* and am pleasantly surprised at the resonance of so many things he says. I go back to old memories. Surely, Calcutta is a moveable feast. I get a feeling that things are changing too fast; soon, nothing will be left of an old world except our memories and then, memories of memories.

Photo: Pradeep Malhotra

That brings me to the question: where am I located, in the here and now or in my memories? What is my reality? Is what I am doing right now and where I am at this moment my only reality or the only reality that matters? And to whom does it matter? Perhaps, only the present moment matters? The past, the future, the other—all these are not in my hands, so what do I have to do with those? Right now, it is only this kitten parked safely on my writing table and the notebook I am writing in and this pen that matter. Also, the crow, the dog and the birds outside that I can hear and Leelu and Kabbu playing somewhere in the background. Perhaps, the sun too, which is out nice and bright, and the breeze, blowing so gently. Do only things that surround me now matter? Do they constitute my reality in the moment?

And now, some sounds of men's voices have entered my reality. Soon, more things tumble into my reality—a rumbling from my hungry stomach, a cry of a child in the neighbourhood, someone working in the kitchen, the sounds of cups and saucers being washed. All this is my ever-growing reality of the moment. It is the reality I am living in. It is the 'is' I must live to the full, for It contains everything. I must not be dreaming of another wishful reality, perhaps located in Africa. Could there just be someone in Timbuktu undertaking a similar, convoluted mental exercise at this moment?

And now, a resounding 'moo' from the neighbour's cow sounds, as if echoing my thoughts. A 'moo' to you too! The kitten has curled up further, oblivious of my deep ponderings of this moment and of what is really real. For her, reality is being curled up on my writing table, in dreamland, with not a kitten care in the world, while I am at my contortionist best reflecting on the reality of the moment, what is and what is not, what is really real and what is not.

Brindavan ka Krishna Kanhaiya

A song echoes from some distance from a temple in our valley at Bhimtal, Kumaon: *'Brindavan ka Krishna Kanhaiya sab ki aankhon ka tara...'* a song that evokes and celebrates Krishna's childhood, his ever-present flute on his lips and a peacock feather in his hair. It reverberates through my being. It has echoed in my mind since I was little, regardless of whether I was happy or sad. Perhaps it was one of the very first songs I was conscious of or had heard. It evoked different images of a childhood imbued with the presence of Krishna. Or was it my very young imagination playing tricks on me?

The experiences of life turned out to be in dramatic and stark contrast to this idyllic imagination, but strangely, this song, this tune, has remained an anthem. Increasingly, with each passing day, I feel the presence of Krishna more and more. He comes unbidden, stealthily, overturning all certainties. The siren call of his flute ensnares, leaving me wondering, and just as suddenly, his presence vanishes along with those mysterious notes of his flute, as if they never were, never existed, were merely figments of my imagination.

O *Krishna,* are you a figment of my imagination? If that is so, let my imagination be. I would rather have you than anything the world has to offer. You, who play hide and seek with our hearts, to you we offer our adoration. All the flowers in the world along with our silent tears are offered at your feet. Open our hearts to an essential truth, to see the world as your play, all that we can see and all that we can't. Open our minds, destroy all barriers, all obstacles, that come in our way. Make all divisions in our hearts, all our constricted ways of being, disappear. May we see all things in some divine light.

May all illusion of our outer lives be dissolved, merged with the one we adore. May we see Krishna in all things and beings, Krishna in time and space, Krishna in life and in death. Let all things shine once again in their original hue, untouched and pure. May our minds and hearts be in an unending flowering of bliss. Let each heart connect to a perennial shower, a golden mist that transcends to a love that knows no bounds, a love that cascades in endless waves, bringing all things into its conscious flow. Supreme harmony, supreme truth, take us with you on this journey to an eternal *ananda*, an eternal felicity.

Is Anything Small?

The sun shines bright in the Kumaon hills. All is well with the world. Birds call from all sides. There are sounds of activity in the kitchen. The hum of cars is heard from far away. A solitary voice calls out. There is a sudden flap of wings in the air. The kitten at the doorway looks up inquiringly and is then off to find its siblings. Now, I hear the mooing of cows, the barking of a dog and then a tinkling sound. I feel the warmth of the sun on my hands. A thought flits by, accompanied by the sound of a school bell. I hear someone calling out and then the hum of a bus picking up speed. They are small sounds, sometimes mixed in a jumble. We need to be quiet to observe the small happenings around us or else, in the rush of life, the beauty of the small, the seemingly insignificant, completely passes us by.

Photo: Pradeep Malhotra

I will be meeting my old friend, Freddie, for lunch. He will be picking me up on his much travelled and battered jeep. My first meeting with his family stands out in my memory. His mother had gifted me a bottle of jam she had made—a small thing, a small gesture, but deeply meaningful. Is anything small? Everything is equally important. 'All life is yoga' as Sri Aurobindo said. This is an essential philosophy of life. Each thing is divine, each moment is divine. We are of divine essence. We are transitional sojourners of divine origin, here on earth with a purpose.

Each person comes with a unique task, which only he or she can do, something special that each has voluntarily chosen. Each comes with his individual talents and predispositions. Each comes with his vision of perfection. It is this divine that we must manifest on earth, through thought, song, action, things small and big. In the divine plan, all things are equally important. Look at the way the Divine has designed the smallest of things—insects, plants, birds—with great love and care, taking care of the minutest details. And look at the beauty—each thing beautifully crafted with all the patience and time in the world, an act of supreme love.

But the Creator is not attached to his creation. Things come, things go, things and beings are manifest, things and beings dissolve once more into the supreme existence—one dramatic scene after another and then an equally dramatic exit. Why then are we intent on holding on to or reducing all things, interpreting all through only a material vision? There could be many ways of seeing the same thing. With our eyes, we see the colours, the shape and the size. With an electron microscope, we can see the underlying structure. With a divine vision, perhaps we may see the underlying relationships of all things under all possible conditions.

Everything is divine, in a state of perennial transformation. Nothing is static; nothing remains the same, not even for a moment.

So, what are we attached to? Can I be attached to what was yesterday or a year ago or maybe even ten years ago? It is only the present that matters, the constantly evolving present. Can we be alert, be in the moment? Can we see in the smallest of things, a transient beauty and joy? Each thing is imbued with a golden transience, every thing!

A World Within a World

I hear birds hidden from sight, chirping away to their hearts' content, seemingly with not a care in the world. A grasshopper, translucent and vivid green, sits crouching, alert, for what seems forever. There is a glint of dew on a cobweb, minute droplets reflecting light. A bird wings its way on the horizon. I hear a faint hum and rumble at some distance, the sound of a bucket scraping the floor and little Kabbu calling out to her sisters. This is my world, my reality of the moment. Also a reality are these pesky flies sitting on my arm.

My thoughts wander, from here to there, everywhere. Where is Leelu? Where is Hemu? I must discuss with them the colour and paint for the doors and windows. I must make a call to my friend, Bhuvan, to check his schedule for tomorrow and speak to Mohan Bhatt at the local *kirana* store for grocery provisions. And yes, I need to return the scarf and cap that I have borrowed. In midst of these thoughts, my littlest neighbour, Ansu, lands at my door with her ever-scampering black dog, Laxy; he gives me a few friendly licks. Now, both head off to find Kerry, our cat.

Each little incident is so full in itself, a world within a world. Little Ansu is now back and commenting on the hair on the back of my hand; she is an observant and talkative handful. In silence, I observe myself in the brief lull as Ansu wanders away, lost in a world of her own. Each of us is lost in worlds of our own, with memories interspersed with desires and some calls or urgencies of the moment…perhaps even some deep longing for a flawless world where all things are as perfect as they are in heaven!

Is there perfection and harmony at the heart of all things, the harmony that we aspire for, awake or asleep? Is harmony hardwired into our very beings, a longing to beat all longings, a perfection with no scope for error, an ultimate precision? Can we ever achieve this? Is this an error of thinking, an aberration and a delusion? Does perfection, a perfect harmony, lie at the heart of creation? Are we but integral units of this evolving perfection? Can someone say? Can someone tell?

This Moment is my Call—Pages from a Kumaon Diary

A warmer day, and thank God for that! We have had a surfeit of cold at our home, 'Dharini' in Bhimtal, Kumaon. A tinkle of bells somewhere announces cows grazing. Little Kabbu and her friends are enjoying their Sunday holiday; their voices can be heard as they flit about. Hema and Leelu have gone to fetch grass and leaves for the cows from Amdali village. They should be on their way back as evening sets in.

Photo: Pradeep Malhotra

The sun shines on my knees with a burning sensation. I wonder why. It brings back memories of school days at 'Sherwood' in Nainital, when we burnt all kinds of things at random. We used a magnifying glass to burn dry leaves and carbon paper, lit bonfires and even burnt our initials into the school's hallowed wooden pillars for posterity. And then, more memories of times past come to the fore—of friends, teachers, others, of experiences that touched me and left their silent traces.

Jim Corbett makes once such memory. I recall the spine-chilling thrill of reading *Man Eaters of Kumaon* one evening as it grew dark. I was safely buttressed by the stone walls of my classroom at 'Sherwood,' which was surrounded by a nice, thick forest where leopards still prowled. His hill abode, 'Gurney House,' was on the way, as we walked to school from Mallital Bazaar along a steep and slowly winding pathway towards Ayarpata Hill.

An introduction to E P Gee's *Wildlife of India* by visiting teacher Hari Dang was an eye opener, an invitation to a vast rich panorama that unfolded before our welcoming eyes. Annual visits by the travelling theatre company *Yatrik* meant we were regaled with plays by Shakespeare and other playwrights. There was no let up to the wild escapades of my favourite hero, fellow brigand and comrade-in-arms, 'William,' as I devoured the Richmal Crompton series. And my house 'Robin Hood' and its colour green played no small role, in keeping with the old Sherwood Forest tradition.

There were unending wet days when the monsoon began, the moist air redolent with leaf, shrub and grass smells that mingled with smoke from nearby wood fires. And I remember a whole army of *langurs* that came every now and then, clambering thunderously on to tin roofs on cold, misty mornings, shaking us out of our dreams and wits. Small things, small incidents but constituting an unforgettable memory of a past long gone.

And then what of all those friends? Paul Sherriff, the first nature enthusiast and rock collector I encountered, who took us through dark, wet caves and crevices to explore stalactites, or was it stalagmites? The brothers Omar and

Hafiz Imam, who just refused to be out of water and swam the entire course of the Naini Lake. 'Uncle' Mehta, the guy who made an art form out of nicking voluminous encyclopaedias from bookstores, while some of us were wholly content with lowly comics! 'Joe' Raina and the Siddhu brothers who tried to blow up a school building, making improvised explosives from chemicals ferreted from the school lab; perhaps, this was a pioneering attempt at de-schooling society!

And teachers? Tiwari, Theo, Ollie, Thapa? 'Than' Thompson with his ever present briar wood pipe at the music block and ancient Blomfield 'Blommy,' who taught us carpentry with quivering hands, while he surreptitiously swigged brandy hidden in *tarpeen* bottles to keep himself steady. He had been Lutyens' assistant on the New Delhi project! And the many other teachers and friends who came and went. Where did they all go? I search for them deep in my heart. Perhaps, they are all there somewhere, untouched, inviolate, held sacred and secure in some universal memory.

The sun turns hot while I sit nibbling on a soft corn, a sweet *bhutta,* from our garden. And Leelu has made some *haldi* pickle for me to carry. I must also take a nice *kakri* that I saw hanging and a very plump *kaddu* that has caught my eye. And some fiery red chillies and lemons and oranges… they smell so fresh, so good. Each little thing, like each little memory, is so vivid, standing out as if saying see, see!

I go into a reverie, a deep feeling that we are approaching some revelation, perhaps a glimmer now widening in scope. Are we, with each passing moment, coming to some uniting of our fragmented selves, closer to the divine that lies within? The day we catch a bigger glimpse, we will not rest till we have seen the Divine in everything—the pebble, the grass, the tree—in all of God's creation, in all of God's moments! I sense in this little moment of revelation something divine in our lovely cats, Sonu and Kerry; in Binduli, our cow; Monu, the calf; in Laxy, the neighbour's dog; in the chattering brotherhood of the *'sat bhai'* or is it the seven sisters, who have come visiting. Each little thing is imbued with its share of immortality, with a bit of wickedness too thrown in. But who are we to judge?

And yes, we are always judging things, from our own little perspectives, whether things suit us or not—do we like their colours and their shapes, and their value, their price in the short and long run, whether we can store them in a bank, in a vault? But can this moment be stored? This shrill cry of an insistent bird, this bark of a dog, this calf calling its mother, this child reaching out to play…right now! Can I respond to tomorrow's calls or those of yesterday? This moment is my call, this very moment. Can I fill this moment with all there is? Can I fill it with eternity?

As evening descends, the sky turns pink-blue. From a distance, I spy a straggling line of hill women trudging along with their precious bundles of leaf and hay. Why, it is Hema, Leelu and our neighbours returning after their day's sojourn. I bring out my camera. As they trudge up to the field, I take a couple of pictures—a mirror to the life of these brave women of the hills. The scene has an enduring, timeless quality as the sun sets and the sky turns a deep pink-blue. They must be truly tired today.

My Friend, the Wandering Pup

My friend, the little puppy, is here. His tail seems to be longer than him! His tail wags and thumps the floor. He gives me a lick and then a friendly nip and ambles off to loll in the sun. I wonder where he has come from, who he belongs to. He seems to have adopted this place. A nice sunny day this, with no sign of the rain predicted when I left Delhi. Our cat calls out somewhere. The pup is back, wanting some bun. He likes his snack, but this is a bit much: he has jumped onto the table and sent my book flying. Sit! Don't look at me with those eyes! No eye contact!

Life delights from moment to moment, if we look at it with new eyes, untouched by the past.

So, what is on my plate at present? Maybe I'll show Hema, our farm-keeper and caretaker's wife, some perennial wild plants growing in our neighbourhood. We can do with some here. Then, I can visit old friends and colleagues at the Children's Village next door and share some news.

And now, this pest is back. What does he want? He is chewing the table leg, tail wagging, and then he growls and snaps at a passing fly.

Look at this pup, so small and portable, yet so full of life! And there… what is that bird that calls from a distance? Just yesterday, I saw a wonderful sight of blue magpies with long tails gliding past gracefully. Narender, the caretaker, has located my long-lost school friend, Vinod of Sanguri

Village. He now lives in Haldwani. I wonder if I will be able to catch up with him sometime soon.

Faint sounds from all over—I can hear each of them if I am quiet. Perhaps, I can even hear the truth of my heart if I am very quiet! A wandering *kabadiwala* calls out in the distance, a call to get rid of one's household junk and get paid for it too! I wonder if it is my old friend, Nassir, the scrap dealer. He has gracefully accepted his lot in life and is doing all that it entails. That perhaps is *karma yoga*!

A thought pops up like some persistent itch—does this have any meaning or is this some reflex long cultivated? The cat calls out, but why? Who or what does she call out to? Answering calls from birds and cows make an erratic symphony. The pup is now asleep at my feet. He has made sure his body is in the sun but his face is in the shade! We need the sun; we always need the sun to feel warm and secure. But then…we need some shade too!

Is There Something we are Unable to see?

This morning's *holi*, the festival of colours, in the Bhimtal, Kumaon hills, has left me with a sense of lazy stupor. The *holi* revelry—with the beating of drums and *pahari* hill songs, sprinkling of colours dry and wet, enjoying *gujiya* and other assorted sweets at every place I halted—has left me a bit weary. There was a small stream of neighbours this morning, youngsters on their way to wilder gatherings and elders on their rounds, visiting friends. The children and neighbours were unrecognisable, with faces smeared in colours of all hues—it was quite a sight.

Photo: Pradeep Malhotra

I take a leisurely a trip to my friend Peter's old, rambling cottage at June Estate through a winding pathway across a wooded hill, photographing whatever I fancy en route—wild flowers, broken branches, discarded tyres on an abandoned rooftop, a rusty old gate. I see a family in a merry, *holi* mood, dancing with gay abandon, their faces unrecognisable with colour. Then, a pleasant greeting exchanged with an Osho-like character, a sage with a deep, flowing beard and a gentle smile.

All along the way, I see signs of devastation—hillsides eroded, rubble strewn, trees and branches laid bare. A thought comes to mind—have we lost all moorings? What we once saw as permanent, lifelong landmarks, I now see crumbling before my eyes. Mountains, vistas, buildings, cultures, communities, identities, everything is in the pot now, everything is up for grabs. I wonder what will come out of this fermenting.

Are we being stewed in juices of our own? Or are we like a caterpillar in the process of being transformed in a not-so-sealed cocoon? What will emerge is the question. Humanity transformed to a new possibility or something stillborn, doomed to an unseasonal exit? And then, yet another question, why would divine wisdom bring us so far and then let go? Is there something we are unable to see, unable to discern? Can our minds go so far and no further? Do we need to silence ourselves, go deeper within? Deep, deep down till we find the Divine once again?

How are we to make this transition? What are the steps? Who is our guide? Or do we travel blindfolded, guided by some deep intuition? Perhaps, once we take a step with faith, the path appears and soon becomes a road. Will the destination then be far away? Can we lock on to the Divine within and ride on regardless? Someone waits for us on the horizon. He waits with open arms and says, have no fear, come home to me.

Seeds Carried by the Wind

My young niece Bia appears for her high school exams today. How time has flown—from her babyhood to her now tentative steps into a more grown-up world! There is trepidation in the hearts of her family and friends, who have seen her grow, about what the future holds, but there is also some knowing that future events will be shaped by how things unfold as a part of a larger plan.

We take all actions that we need to, but we try and keep in mind that only the Divine has the full picture. We must go deep within to intuit this big picture; it will save us from many a pitfall. Time and again, 'my will and desire' is pitted against this big picture that providence has prepared for us. Parents, friends and teachers are all part of this big picture.

An all-seeing wisdom and vision guides Bia and each of us if only we let ourselves be guided, if we consent to being shown the way. The way lies in quieting our outer minds and letting a small, inner voice paint before us an integral picture of an evolving, dynamic possibility, a wave on which to ride. The emerging adult must explore, search, navigate. She may start with a small ambit and bit-by-bit weave in and out to move to larger realms.

The young student should be a bit of an adventurer in search of a pot of gold. The adventure may lead to many surprises, false trails and even dead ends. It will lead to big breakthroughs too. The exploration and the adventure is the seed for what is to follow. It is a refining of purpose, a widening of horizons, a broadening of consciousness itself. And when we are fully conscious, where are the barriers, the confusion? We become focused all the way through.

Every young person needs a liberal, extensive education, an education the child points to and gifts herself. It is an education tailor-made to the spiritual needs of the child, in harmony with the child's unique identity and personal journey. It helps in rounding, connecting and making fuller all the latent talents waiting to burst forth like seeds from a pod, which will be carried by the wind to a spot that is fertile and nurturing.

Let each child be given this opportunity to become who and what it is in its essential nature, to fulfil the bigger picture; anything less distorts the divine plan. Each child must soar and attain great heights and from those heights see its own role, divinely ordained and unique, perfectly suited to the task at hand. We wish Bia bon voyage.

Ephemeral, Yet Imbued with Eternity

Our cow, Binduli, at our home, 'Dharini,' is unwell. It breaks one's heart to see animals suffer. They take it in their stride; there is a stoic acceptance of what is. Is there a lesson in this for us too? Life will bring with it joys and sufferings and we need to accept things as they come. Binduli needs to be shown to the vet and will; so too, at times, will each of be ill, face problems, need a doctor. We make all efforts, do one's duty, say a prayer, and then…let go. What will be, will be!

Photo: Pradeep Malhotra

Our crisis today is that we want only our wills to be, only my will to be. We are not prepared to listen to an eternal will whose music is always in the air. Our ears are closed to the call of its harmony. But then, at times, a little note from seemingly nowhere deeply enthrals. A spell that had so negatively enveloped us is broken and once again, we hear heaven's music—a small note, but with the promise of a symphony to follow. Suddenly, we are alert to new possibilities. Our individual crisis, the world's crisis, may yet be an opportunity.

The words of the Mother, Mirra Alfassa, echo in my mind—her words describing her state, her consciousness becoming 'contagious,' while bringing down the supramental consciousness into the earth body. Is it the sounds of this contagion that we hear today masquerading as clash and clamour, confusion, uncertainty, babel, an end of civilisation? Perhaps it is the end of things as we have always known them. But endings are new beginnings too. Could this confusion we see be the forerunner of a new way of seeing and doing things? Perhaps, it brings with it seeds of a new dawn, fresh and open.

Perhaps, the evolving new man will not be man but a new consciousness; free to go where a small heavenly note beckons, evolving endlessly, to endless possibilities. No chains any more, just free. Nothing 'me' or 'mine' anymore, everything belonging to everyone, even my body not mine, but being one with everything. The world's pain is my pain. All its ills are mine. Its present throes and pangs are mine. The hurt of a butterfly hurts me. The tears of a child make me weep. The pain of an animal is my own pain. The world is interconnected, bodies are interconnected…we are one consciousness.

Thousands of years ago, the Buddha had pointed to a co-arising taking place, a co-evolution. Either we evolve to a new consciousness or we perish, to start from scratch yet again. Nature can wait. It can try again and again, but our own time spans are limited, ephemeral. Let us not waste the moment. Let us follow the eternal path as it reveals itself moment by moment with courage and the certainty of its victory.

Coincidence or Hide and Seek?

Coincidences can be lovely! Last evening, I was witness to two. A few hours after I picked up a book on Salvador Dali, I encountered a crossword on his life in an evening paper. Later in the day, I bumped into my friends, Satish and Rati, after years, on my walk near the Bhimtal Lake; they were here for a short holiday. I had been thinking of them and needed to be in touch again. How do such things happen? Does our subconscious mind somehow participate in making these things happen? Or is it that when we are particularly sensitive, we consciously observe a phenomenon that is happening all the time?

And if it is, it seems we are blind to things for a major portion of our lives, just occasionally getting a glimpse into another world lying totally hidden. Is it a game of hide-and-seek? Who is hiding and what are we seeking? Or is it that we are hiding and are the ones sought? Intriguing possibilities! What activates our intuition at times and what keeps it dormant? A deep quest for something and a silent mind seem to be contributing factors. The answers to our quest are there, but hidden in a maze. We must run the gauntlet of the maze to encounter the clues. But clues are apt to be missed if we are not careful, if we walk too fast, if our eyes wander too soon, if the mind is too full of other things. With a silent mind, we can unravel the entire plot. One thing leads to another.

We always seem to forget that everything is interconnected. We are one consciousness. The world is one, the universe is one. When a child smiles, my heart smiles too; when someone dies in Syria, in Lebanon, in Kashmir… a part of me dies too; when an animal is in pain, I am in pain too—like attracts like. My foremost thoughts link me to things I value most. They will emerge sooner than later from the unlikeliest of places—hidden, mysterious encounters, miracles in every nook and corner!

As I take a stroll, there are encounters, coincidences, intuitive occurrences. Life begins to flow as if in a dream. Is God dreaming and are we collaborators and participants in his dream? Often, we forget that this is hide-and-seek of a high order and are bewildered, lost, at our wits' end. Life loses its charm and we have a taste of ashes; the clock seems to have stopped for good.

And then there is a break, a sudden change. Another element, hidden, but full of potential, silently makes an entry. Every detour has a meaning, so does every delay. The detour may delay us but does that mean we will not reach our goal? Perhaps, the delay will round off the edges, smooth the passage. Perhaps, it will ward off a disaster. Who knows? Haste makes waste; let us slow down a bit. We then get more time to see the scenery. We can also pause to get some fresh air or dawdle awhile at a pretty scene, or play a game with a child, or chase a butterfly or maybe even pursue a rainbow. We may even discover what lies at the end of the rainbow. Perhaps, a golden stream that leads straight up to heaven!

Let it Go...Let it Flow

Does this pen work? @#*! Perhaps, it requires some persistence; perhaps, the ink is frozen. Surprising? Not so. This pen is a memento from Sweden! I guess mementos should be kept as mementos and nothing more. They commemorate some pleasant interlude or the other. But writing like this is not very pleasant. Let me switch to another pen.

Some pens just do not work. Can we keep flogging a dead horse? That is cruelty. We still live in an old mindset with memories of things long past. This pen, this situation, does not work anymore but the memory of some past association with it compels me to keep trying. Let go! Try using something else. If one thing does not work, something else will. Try and try again.

Photo: Pradeep Malhotra

The whole of evolution is about trying and trying again. Nature persists despite all odds. It is tireless in its efforts. No matter what, it keeps persisting in trying to achieve its goal of a constantly evolving perfection. It wants its creation to be in harmony with itself. With the crudest of materials, it shapes the most subtle of results. These subtle perfections are but a crude raw material for its next effort.

Look at the ages of man. Today, we have reached an electronics age surpassing all revolutions of old. We already sense that this age is only a prelude of what is to come next. Communication has annihilated time and space. We are all one now, each connected to the other. I sneeze and the world catches a cold; you laugh and the world is full of smiles. We are contagious. The world is in the grips of a new contagion. All the old laws stand subverted. This is a new quicksand. The old logic no longer works and we are yet to grasp a new one.

The contours of a new logic are beginning to appear, small flecks on the horizon, so small that they are barely perceptible. They glimmer here and there, and if you try to look too closely, they are gone—ephemeral! You can't hold on to this new logic. You can only be in it. You flow with its flow.

The spoilers to this show are many: grains of sand that get into the eyes, which get into our very beings. They deflect, turn us around 360 degrees, one dead end after another. And it is only at the dead end that one's eyes open once again. What is it that lies on the horizon? Is it a mirage? Or could it be a wonderful oasis? Is it a new creation, a new consciousness? Perhaps, it is a brand new pen that really works.

A Beacon for the Truth that is Everywhere

A chill wind blows in our valley and I have a cold and a fever, but I make the best of this languid evening by watching *Lincoln* on my laptop, with a cup of hot tea by my side. It is a great film with a nice period flavour, directed by Steven Spielberg and Daniel Day-Lewis playing Lincoln. The director takes you back in time by shooting under gas and lamp light.

Was Abraham Lincoln the tallest and greatest of American presidents? For me, perhaps no one came quite as close to him, except Jimmy Carter, in terms of a spiritual bonding. What stood out in Lincoln was his deep feeling for his fellow man and quiet spirituality. What I had not known was another side to him that was very human, mischievous, yet determined. He could go to any lengths to achieve his goals, subterfuge and underhand technique included! The film focuses on Lincoln's efforts in 1865 to have the Thirteenth Amendment to the Constitution passed by the House of Representatives to end the slave trade and make sure that those freed were not enslaved again.

A soulful, mysterious and intriguing character with a hidden sorrow circling his eyes—who was he really? What was his greater evolutionary role? I must get to know more. Our souls move from life to life; where would Lincoln be today? I sense a co-evolution taking place, consciousness touching consciousness, evolving with each contact that is made lifetime after lifetime.

Would a man such as Lincoln succeed in today's age or would he be a misfit, his size not quite fitting anything? He was ahead of his times; perhaps today too he would be ahead, steadily working towards the fundamental equality of all things and beings. The United States has changed much since that Civil War; the entire landscape, ways of life, ways of being, everything has changed. Yet, at the core, what has really changed? The same questions have re-emerged, at times with even greater force, but now in a newer context— the same fundamental quest for an inner and outer equality.

Has the United States carried forward Lincoln's dream, the essence of his dreams and aspirations? Or has it been in outward substance only? Are there two Americas, one of outward appearances and another hidden from sight? When will hidden America take on its rightful role? When will a silent, spiritual America come to the forefront? When will the spirit of its indigenous people get full voice again? When will its migrant millions be one in spiritual quest? When will America be one with the universal dream?

The time does not seem far. Seeds wait for the right moment to sprout. Does a fire await America, an eternal fire that burns in every heart? Will America flower yet again? Not to dominate but to shine, a living demonstration of a truth that awaits us—a beacon for the truth that is everywhere.

A Story you would have Never Heard

What story can I tell, I wonder. Something that might have happened or that might not have? Can a story be plucked out of ones hat? What of all those strange happenings that still make my heart miss a beat? Then again, I wonder what the truth was and what was the work of imagination. Strange happenings, whose purpose I am not sure about…to take us to another truth, to another world?

Photo: Pradeep Malhotra

'One dark night, when the wind blew icy cold on a lonely mountain hill, cut off, far away…'

That dark night has its story to tell, perhaps a story within a story. We live in many worlds simultaneously, one seen and acknowledged and others hidden, whose glimpse we get rarely. Such glimpses come perhaps in those special moments when we are receptive or vulnerable or when our senses are heightened, when we are open to anything. And when we are, anything can happen. But on that dark, cold, damp night, did it really happen? What really happened? I cannot really say.

This world is not only what we see with our naked eye. This world is neither what we hear, nor what we touch and feel; it is that too, but much, much more. There are layers within layers, truths within truths, diamonds within diamonds—their reflected rays touching one another, their beauty amplified and multiplied. All things are singing praise to some hidden truth, always awaiting yet another revelation. The superficial event is only the outer form; some inner reality holds the key.

So, what about my story of that dark, mysterious night when it blew icy cold? What story can I tell? The story will only be the outer shell of another reality. The story can be seen in many ways, from many angles, each having its own truth to tell. The same event seen through many eyes, one murder with many sides to the truth. Shades of *Rashomon*! A virtual Pandora's Box that might make Pandora shudder too!

Every man, every thing, has its story to tell. But a happening can never be seen the same way, nor a story told the same way twice. Something would have changed, maybe the storyteller's perception. Perhaps, mine has…did I really see those things? Did all that really happen? Or even perhaps the listener's as well, as he listens. Now even the cast of characters play sudden tricks in the retelling. There is no one truth to a story. There is no one story to what happened that grim, dark night.

And all those things that had happened, all those things that I had seen and felt? What of those? Were they real or were they figments of my imagination? Do I then live in some make-believe, dream world that has no essential reality? Is reality whatever we choose to make of it? Good and evil, black and white, high and low, life and death? Is reality a choice of antagonisms, a mix of contradictions, concocted in whatever proportions of one's choice, blended to perfection?

So, what of my story, of that grim, dark, sinister night which took many darker turns?

Can we take in a bit of this and a bit of that, and then a bit of everything? Then mix them, churn them, bring them to a boil and lay them on a platter? No, that would not be fair, to you, to me, to those things that once happened. So, this is my story. I am still figuring it out, trying to make something of that dark, damp night when nothing made sense. Did it really happen? What really happened? Every story has many sides to it; there is no single truth.

Would you take it or leave it? Perhaps you would like some more garnish, some toppings. I have them. But believe me, this is a story you would have never heard before. So, let me try again. 'One dark night, when the wind blew icy cold on a lonely mountain hill, cut off, far away...'

The Girl from Harappa...or is it Mohenjo-Daro?

I remember this figurine. It is perhaps from the Harappa period. I had picked it up from the souvenir shop when I did studies in Art at the National Museum. How fresh and vibrant it had looked despite the centuries that had passed. The girl's hair was braided in exquisite twirls and with ornaments; she had curved eyelids and wore a bold *bindi* on her forehead that would put a modern woman to shame. Was she a woman far ahead of her times? Or was perhaps the sculptor?

Today, this figure stands chipped as a result of a fall from my hands. Perhaps, I can touch it with a bit of colour, some clay and then a dab of black on the patches at the base. Then, I notice influences, traces of another period, but I can't quite place my finger…let me check my dates and history again!

So it is with many things on my table—each has a history of its own, things fresh, hand-picked at some given moment, and now forgotten, waiting to tell their stories. Yes, things should be moved around every now and then. You can see them from a new perspective, with fresh new eyes. Perhaps they may have some fresh new story to tell, some fresh new world to create.

Now, I see this same figure from one side: what lustrous hair this woman had, thick like a dense forest. Could it just be possible that she was wearing a bun or wig? The sculptor too was entitled to his imagination. And then some vandal moment lopped off an entire dimension from her body, her torso! With time, only some fragment was left; the body, heart and soul had been consumed by time. What we see now is a shadow of some former self. Even in that shadow are exquisite lines and forms, beauty and an ephemeral vanity that left its mark.

This was a full and pulsating life, brimming with energy and desire, invincible till it lasted, a touch of the eternal reflected in its confident poise. Through the ages, it communicates some message, but I wonder what? Perhaps, that all things shall pass. Youth shall pass. Beauty shall pass. The outer shell, life, shall pass. But the idea of eternal youth and beauty shall stay on forever.

It's Christmas!

It's Christmas! This winter day has a white Christmas feel. It is a day of great promise, from God to man and man to God.

Today, the car has broken down. A mechanic has come to repair it. One problem solved has led to the discovery of yet another. And to top it, the electricity has gone and the help won't be coming. When does this catch-22 end? We seem to have a back-to-back program as far as problems go. Life doesn't seem to leave us with much of a choice. It says choose this or that. I choose that. And it says, now again, choose this or that. Life seems to be playing snakes and ladders with us all the time. The choice is bread and jam with a lot of sand in it or sand with a teeny-weeny bit of bread and jam thrown in. I say it is more snakes than ladders. Snakes must be getting fatter!

Photo: Pradeep Malhotra

Here's Christmas and we are talking of snakes and ladders. I would rather think of friends and music this evening, of carols, wine and cake—a nice plum cake with cherry toppings!

Perhaps, we can we have wine and cake and invite the whole world to the party, animals, birds and plants included. And we can go dressed as each other. It will be a wild, wild party. And God? He will be the chief guest. But we do have a big problem here. What does the chief guest like to eat and drink? Does he like wine and plum cake? That's the trouble with parties—you have to cater to every taste.

And yes, I quite forgot, what will he come dressed as? How do we know it is God? He could come disguised as a whale or as an Amazonian butterfly. Or even a ptarmigan. He could come in as a rose plant or as a peacock. He could come as a cedar tree or a kangaroo. He could come as you or me. Or he could come as a baby.

And once, he actually did. Jesus came to us as a baby. And there was a party that night. The stars were out, shining nice and bright. The wise men came and animals too. There was quite a hullabaloo.

The effects of that night's party are still with us. Some hangover! We haven't got over the message Christ brought with him: the cheer and the peace and God's love for man. He also brought with him man's path to the future. A path strewn with rocks, stones and thorns, but only if we see the outer surface. Inside and below, hidden very craftily, lie rubies, gold and emeralds. A treasure the likes of which we have never seen, nor can imagine.

But he likes to play hide and seek and snakes and ladders. What is a party without all the games—blind man's bluff, bingo, musical chairs! What fun! Some tears too, some big heartbreaks en route. Sometimes even a wild, wild country ride, right to the very top, to the majestic Himalayas, to Mt Everest itself!

And now... what a grand, grand view! A view of the world with perspective...of life, as seen from all sides. So, that's what it was all about!

PS: I went dressed as Edmund Hillary. Do you think it could have been God disguised as Sherpa Tenzing Norgay sitting next to me?

Merry Christmas!

Holy Bananas—New Age Nirvana!

Everyone is out to make a fast buck, no matter how. Is it in our genes? Did God put it into evolution for a purpose—making a fast buck, getting something for nothing or for very little, getting much more than our investment? Like a robber who robs but gives nothing in return. Perhaps, he gives something too, a rather expensive lesson to the one robbed. So, is robbery in our bones?

The birds do it, robbing other birds' nests. The bees do it, robbing poor flowers. And then, animals prey on other animals! Everyone wants to get something for nothing. But some might say that there is quite some effort in all this; look at the skulduggery involved! And once you make a fast buck, how do you keep it safe without another scoundrel making off with it? It's an endless cycle, with the only democratic plus point being the many fingers in the process, sharing what was thought to be a very exclusive pie. So, is there some method to this madness? Let me try to unravel some secrets…there should be quite a few takers as everyone wants to get his share.

Where do I start to make my fast buck? What scam has been left untouched so far? Let me see. Perhaps, I can surreptitiously sell the North Korean Slam-Bam-Bam and Mudz-On-U very dirty missile secrets to the Americans. It would solve everyone's problems and no one would get nuked. Americans get the very un-clear North Korean technology, exchanged by the Chinese, re-exchanged by the Pakistanis, overseen, with one eye firmly shut, by the Americans themselves; or is it some other way around? North Koreans get prestige by fooling and cocking a snook at Americans and showing themselves top hot dog with red chili sauce because they have the super stinker Gobor-Dung missile hidden up their sleeve. The world breathes a big sigh of relief, and I breathe two, as I make some very fat bucks. Everyone is happy! Now, let me ponder the many other ideas trickling down my brain.

We now have many win-win-win solutions and everyone is a winner! The trouble is, we have been looking at things from the wrong end of the barrel. Fast buck power flows from the right end of the barrel, provided you clearly know which the right end is. Every solution has a problem, a case of reverse engineering. We just need to identify these. Now, just imagine we have global think-tanks dedicated to problem creation for solutions that are already there. Can anything be faster or quicker?

Perhaps, this is God's way of giving us *nirvana* on the quick. He has tried the old methods, but those took billions of years and there were no sure-fire results. And now, our new consciousness has an instant answer: you get the goodies before you can even say 'holy bananas'; you spend the buck even before you have stolen it!

HONEYBEES IN SEARCH OF GOLD

Led by a sacred flame

All things are interconnected, finely woven and imperceptible to all but the Creator. A fine tapestry of hidden lines and forms, intricate arrangements, crafted with unsurpassed precision. Thin, microscopic veins running through the universe, crisscrossing along galaxies and continents, undercurrents, waves and infinitesimal pulls and pressures in every direction—the many forms of the divine energy that create, energise, mobilise and destroy. A Divine *Shakti* does her will, chooses her scenes to play.

Photo: Pradeep Malhotra

She is the calm of the mighty sea, the rumble of the volcano. She is the eye of the watchful eagle soaring majestically in the sky. She is the cry of the new-born, the gentle touch of the mother. She is the lumbering stride of the majestic elephant, king of all he surveys. She is the flitting butterfly floating from flower to flower. She is the bee that stings even as she sips nectar that soothes our wounds. She is the mighty torrential river as it winds its way. She is the Ganga that washes away our sins. She is the siren call of beauty that furthers evolution through desire. She is the hidden dream in each heart that makes us aspire. She is the beginning, middle and end of all things.

O Mother Divine, take us on your eternal path, show us the way. May we wayfarers not be lost forever. O Mother, lead us with your luminous light. O Mother, guide our footsteps, enlighten our minds so that we may do your will at each moment. May each step we take be led by your flame hidden in our hearts—sacred, supreme. O Mother Divine, forsake us not for even a moment, see us through our errors and transgressions. With each step take us towards divine delight.

Abide with Me

As the sun sets and evening shadows darken, the notes of Mahatma Gandhi's favourite hymn come wafting into my mind: 'Abide with me; fast falls the eventide; / The darkness deepens; Lord with me abide. / When other helpers fail and comforts flee, / Help of the helpless, O abide with me'.

As the sun goes into hiding, one's mind is at low ebb. As the sun's bright rays, which have brought life to our world through the day, mellow and fade away, so does something in our hearts. At all times, we wish to cling to its life-giving energy and to its light, which dispels the darkness of our minds. We pray, we implore to the Creator, to the divine sun within, to slay the darkness of our being and to bring it on the path of light, of enlightenment.

Does evening and night reflect our weaknesses and fears? Does night resonate with the pitch-black fears of our being? We fear the night just as we love the day. We want it to be daylight forever; bright lights and bulbs are testimony. But what is day without night, light without dark? One cannot exist without the other. The one does not mean anything without the other. The dark contains the seed of light and light contains the seed of dark. Just as the sun sets for us here, it lights the world at the other end—giving to all, unstinting in its benevolence.

We, too, must be like the sun, dynamos of silent action, ever sure of the light in us, whatever the circumstances. Just as the sun's light is but briefly eclipsed for us to rest, so too, we must, in our mind's eye, know that the divine light and love are always with us. Life is an endless flow of light, of enlightenment, that floods every dark nook in existence. Every pore, every cell, in our being is at each moment being filled with this light and love. We, in turn, must, always, be open to receive it. We aspire to this light, we pray for it to enter the very core of our beings, to transform our existence, to take us on an ever-widening spiral of consciousness.

'Lead kindly light,' implores our soul—a prayer to our divine Creator to take us from the unreal to the real, from darkness to immortality. Through the sun, we have the assurance from the Lord of all, of this inner reality, of the light that already is. We pray for it to manifest in our life, in our daily workings, hour by hour, moment by moment, through night and through day. 'Heaven's morning breaks, and earth's vain shadows flee; / In life, in death, O Lord, abide with me'.

Sunday Mornings at Sri Aurobindo Ashram

Sunday mornings, how I look forward to them. To be at Sri Aurobindo Ashram, New Delhi, taking a walk down the 'Sunlit Path' that encircles a vast green expanse of playground, and is full of sunshine. I have done its rounds for many years, yet each time, I feel a fresh burst of energy. The ashram is a place of renewal, a place where sunshine touches every pore of my being. Has the divine given us this very special space? Perhaps, it is an answer to a strong yearning for a space far away from the crowded and stifling—pure, untouched, where our aspirations can mount, where the sun can pour into every little crevice of our being, cleansing and nurturing simultaneously.

Photo: Pradeep Malhotra

And then to spend time listening to a talk or *bhajans,* devotional songs, at the meditation hall or browsing over books and buying incense at the Sabda bookstore or lingering over the *samadhi* that enshrines Sri Aurobindo's relics, in an atmosphere that is tranquil and serene. I watch children practice volleyball or cricket on the playing field. A new patch is being planted elsewhere and each plant and vibrant flower seems to aspire to the divine. I saw Mirambika free progress school in an absolutely new light some days ago and sense the Mother's presence embedded at its very core. It is a blessing to be a child growing up in its environs. Has the child in me been given another chance, an opportunity to see things afresh? To see a new opening, for the coming of a new age of everlasting youth, for minds fresh and open to new possibilities at each moment.

Now, I hear a flutter of wings in the air—doves and pigeons calling out and squirrels chasing each other. A peahen with her chicks in tow crosses my path without fear, trusting and free. Is this the new world waiting to be born, unhindered and fearless? Are these the children of the future who will topple all walls, all barriers? Are these barriers waiting to be toppled without our knowledge? Is a toppling of all obstructions already underway?

But what do we see on the surface of our day-to-day existence? We see a world in chaos, a world reeling in confusion and anger, with attacks and retribution. Where are we headed? Is this an accelerated evolution? Is this an evolutionary crisis and a tipping point? Will we make it through this crisis of crises? There are movements in all directions, a rumble of war and a conjoining of evils. Look at India, look at the world. We sense a reckless speeding gone out of hand. Is anyone listening? A cyclonic movement is gaining momentum—fast, faster money, desires, grab, accuse and defend. Are all days going to be like this?

It is a full circle. We may be coming to the end of a full circle. The world is being connected, everything with everything. There is no 'other'. We remember our teachers who saw the 'world as lover, world as self'. How compassionate their teachings have been! Their compassion flows down the ages. Their enlightenment touches us all. A deep co-arising is seen, all the dots are getting connected! India seen through the eyes of a satellite celebrating *Deepawali,* the festival of lamps and lights, is a nation brightly lit, en-lightened. Let this divine light enter our hearts, our minds, our very existence!

Each Moment Linked
to the Divine

February 21 is the birthday of The Mother, Mirra Alfassa, and *Darshan Day*—a day for a glimpse and vision of divinity. We pray for an opening, a breakthrough in the deep crisis that our country, and the world, is facing. She, in her far-seeing vision, had seen the evolving world situation and its progression. Each of her utterances is crystal clear, on the consequences of our present materialistic trajectory and the practical steps to be taken to move out of this dilemma and into a harmonious and divine future.

Darshan Day is an opportunity to take a deep look at our day-to-day lives in the light of the Mother's guidance. While we are deeply touched by her message, have we been able to assimilate it in our lives? Her message sparkles like crystal, throwing light on the problems of existence. She points to the 'sunlit path,' which though strewn with many difficulties, is the most doable of all. Other paths are beyond the reach of the ordinary man and would need many lifetimes to achieve. Her central message, as I have understood it, has been to show that man has just one mission—to live for the divine, to live in the divine and to see all things in that light.

If we have accepted this message in our hearts, why do we have so much trouble putting it into action in our lives? Why do pulls and pressures and desires thwart the direction we want to take, we must take? Our lives are a dichotomy between what we must be and what we presently are. What is the way out? How do we get out of this predicament we ourselves have created?

Perhaps, things need to be done in small, doable ways. Let us not imagine a 'spiritual life' or the 'supramental' and say 'not doable' in this lifetime. Let us only do one thing at a time. Let us live in minute-tight compartments, second-tight compartments. Let us do what this minute, this second, demands and nothing more. And then, the next minute, the next second—one moment at a time. Let us not bog ourselves down with the thoughts of years and centuries. Just one minute, just one second, is enough. And then that minute, that second, is full of possibility. That second is linked to eternity, to consciousness, to the divine. Each moment is part of that divine consciousness. We treat each moment with love and reverence. We become one with the divine moment.

We strive for a constant remembrance of the divine, at each moment, a conscious remembrance of the divine. A movement towards the divine consciousness under all circumstances, to see the divine in people, things, events and happenings, more so at this present moment, when all seems in a state of disorder, chaos and collapse; this is important to remember at this present moment.

A Moment Sparkling Fresh...Just Born

An intriguing chessboard table-top is my writing desk. It is a new environment that feels vibrant; the day's events are fresh and evolving. This trip to Chandigarh, this tour, has a certain vigour and freshness to it. Why is it that we have such a feeling of freshness and clarity only at times? Why do we not have it in an on-going fashion? Does a sense of newness lie in the unexpected or in the unusual? And new is in the sense of really invigorating, everything sparkling and vibrating—faces, roads, interactions. Not the usual, the mundane, the everyday. We are ready to accept whatever the moment brings.

Photo: Pradeep Malhotra

Can we bring this freshness into our lives from moment to moment? Not to live in the past, but in the now, the right now? Our eyes untouched by the past, not looking into the future, just looking at right now. Eyes that melt into the 'right now,' eyes that are open to the moment everywhere and every time. There is no expectation of what the next moment will bring or even a knowing. Just 'being' with what is in the moment. We live moment to moment, with clarity, with simplicity, untouched by the past or the future.

I see a cloud drifting in the sky. It has no special preferences. It is shaped and moulded by the moment, by what the moment wants, by what the Divine wants in the moment. It is in the service of the Divine, a helper of the Divine. It has no ego. There is no me or mine, it has become part of an unrolling of the divine will, an unrolling of a divine consciousness, a consciousness constantly unrolling, unravelling what it has to.

It is a consciousness that like a long-winged bird soars across continents of time and space, transcending. It is our millions of bodies of consciousness touching each other—mineral, plant, animal, man—that collaborate in a vast note. Maybe even a small one, a little golden note that is absolutely pure. It is a note from the very heart of things, from the very heart of existence—a note of love, of truth, of beauty, with no dissonance, only a flowing harmony. It is a note that is pure, crystal clear, unsullied by time, untouched by thought. Fresh, sparkling fresh, just born!

Why are we Attached to Permanence?

I stroll through long familiar haunts, ambling along old pathways where once much-loved buildings stood. Today, the same spaces are unrecognisable. The old landmarks have gone; there is now a vast expanse with materials strewn and some wild profusion of greenery too. How things change with time! I had thought these landmarks were forever. Time alone tells us nothing is forever. The things I see today may not be there tomorrow. Enduring associations dissolve in the flash of a blink. Ideas that we held so dear are now relics of a bygone age. Everything is transitory, moving, evolving, and so are we.

Why are we so attached to permanence? Why are we unhinged at the thought of transience? All evolution, after all, is an exercise in transience. While the cosmos is engaged in evolving, what are a few decades to eternity? Or are we perhaps eternal beings longing to return to our eternal moorings? Why have we been moved from our eternal home to a transient camp? This is the question troubling the heart of man.

Man wants all things to be eternal—people, relationships, all that we see, even life itself. In God's heart, all things are—every thing, moment or event that ever existed or happened is fresh and immortal in the eyes of the Divine; nothing ever dies. It is an eclipsing of our vision. It is as if our spectacles have changed, from transparent, to coloured, to opaque. What is true and eternal will remain true and eternal. Perhaps obscured, hidden, but still there.

The Divine loves each of its creations, yet is not attached to any. Look at the meticulous way in which each thing is created, from the microscopic to the gigantic, with love and patience. Yet, God is not perturbed when things and beings complete their appointed cycles. Each consciousness merges once again into the eternal, like the stream into the river, the river into the sea. These waters come back once again as rain. Is consciousness then a process, a cyclical movement, a bringing back to itself, a refining of all that comes its way?

Things that were unconscious now become conscious. We, who were asleep, are opening our eyes. As we open our eyes, there is a glimmer of understanding. Maybe we are not who we seem to be. Could we be divine beings in transition? Are we doing yoga and a task for the Divine? A task and yoga, to make life on earth divine.

Everything Lies within Me

Go by intuition, by your gut feelings. Do not be pressurised into situations. Intuition and feelings lead to harmonious outcomes. With intuition, you go with the flow. You are not fighting currents but harmonising with them. Your heart must be in the things that you do. The saddest comment is 'my heart was not in it'. Go where your heart takes you, not on flights of fancy but in actions firmly rooted in what you truly believe—actions that are effortless.

Photo: Pradeep Malhotra

It takes a while to start trusting one's feelings and intuition, perhaps because they are so fleeting and intangible. We are used to a world of hard facts and action, where everything must be measured, quantified and verified and made into a commodity, something of worth, that can be bought or sold or saved and put into a bank locker. All life is seen as a series of transactions to gain the most profit.

Life becomes coarse and hardened and the world becomes an arid landscape, an inferno.

Is it perhaps time to take a U-turn, move a radical 360 degrees? We have seen the future. We do not want what the old thinking will bring. We want life, not death. We want the spirit to live as the master of all it sees or does. The same spirit pervades all—stone, plant, animal and man. It pervades the earth, the planets and galaxies, all of creation.

It is this spirit that wants to be heard; its time of banishment is over. It wants to be in the forefront. It wants to be heard in our thoughts, in the cry of a child, in the call of the tiger to its mate, in the little sapling trying to emerge from the ground, in the thundercloud, in a symphony orchestra and in a life ebbing away. It wants to be heard in everything! Each thing is sacred to it, each moment blessed. Everything has evolved from the sacred—we have only the sacred touching the sacred, love touching love, bliss touching bliss.

Our hearts and minds sense a charade, a cosmic game of deception, where things are not what they first seem to be. The person we had always thought of as an enemy turns out to be a friend. All that you were running away from was all that you always wanted. Heaven was always here. It was here, right in your heart, closer than your closest companion. Yet, you pursued it in everything else you could think of. You pursued in vain. You searched the Himalayas, the densest forests; you went over skies and under the sea. You went to other planets. Yet, you could not see.

Everything lies within you, within me.

'Coming Home'—Looking Back on the Kumbh Mela

Returning from the Kumbh Mela, I look back. What did the journey mean, if anything at all? A greater force had brought each of us to the Kumbh at Allahabad, mixing us with a great stream of life, a stream parallel with its flowing waters. The Kumbh has an amazing diversity of colours, ways of life and languages. Boats move gracefully, a sea of tents harbours people from across the country and the world, men, women, and children, all submerging themselves in a greater consciousness. Each individual path had led to a greater one. A cry of delight broke out the moment we entered the confluence of the waters with their merging hues—*'Har har Gange'* arose the cry in unison in supplication to the Ganga. Each became one with the masses gathered, one body moving towards one goal, towards a *darshan*, a glimpse of the Divine.

Photo: Pradeep Malhotra

One was struck by the simplicity of the gathering, of the ritual performed: a washing of the dust gathered over a lifetime, an aspiration for truth and divinity to enter our lives. It was a cry seeking blessings for the whole world, for all creation, for all those who had left this world, for those presently on the earthly journey, and for those preparing to come. It was a prayer in the heart for a new beginning for all sentient beings.

I saw an amazing kindness and a welcome on every lip. An unending mass of men and women were on a singular quest. Ash-smeared sadhus in ochre, itinerant communities, little children playing with vibrancy and energy on the riverfront asking for a little something, the cows, the dogs, the water birds, were all a part of the landscape that asked for so little. A prayer in my heart asked for the Divine's blessings to shower on all creatures, great and small. But what is great and what is small? All of us are part and parcel of a universal consciousness.

Can we be aware of this special moment, a moment when we are truly becoming conscious, this moment when layer after layer of ourselves and the dark recesses of our minds is being exposed to the divine rays of the sun? It is a moment that is blinding and terrifying, yet, one that we must trust and go forward. We must trust the deepest part of ourselves which is inexorably linked with the Divine, which is part and parcel of the Divine, which is the Divine itself.

It is this divine that is manifesting. It is taking myriad shapes as it manifests, fluid and dynamic, reaching out to everything, taking all in its warm and loving embrace. All is one and there is no other. All of us are children of the one Divine; they follow the call of the divine flute. 'You had all dispersed and gone your ways, but now is the time to come home'. *Ganga Maiya* beckons, Mother Ganga calls out to her children. 'It is getting late. Come home. There is a wonderful feast waiting. Come home.'

A Golden Contagion

The fragrance of incense smoke fills the air. Its wafting smell promises that all is well with the world. It promises wholeness, nurture and divine protection. With our worship, we bring our love. We worship with incense, with flowers, with our tears, with our aspiration. When we aspire deeply for the Divine and yearn intensely, we break barriers. Things become whole again; there is no me and you, this and that, high and low. Everything becomes one again, with all barriers gone. Everything is one, whole, divine, beautiful. The mind is in ecstasy.

All days should begin with a prayer and an aspiration, a prayer to remind ourselves who we really are and why we are here. Our aspiration should take us back to our real, authentic selves, to an eternal process and then help us to live this authenticity. But we are ever forgetful. To forget this truth takes but a moment, the very second our mind is diverted to another task. Within a moment, it becomes the very opposite of the sublime essence that it is.

The same mind is now clouded and deluded. The jaguar claws of the world, its wants and desires grip us in its firm, vicious clasp. Its teeth sink deep to tear out every pound of flesh it claims as its own. Is the mind a fiend of high order, a mischief maker par excellence? Is it a killer machine? It is a sharpened blade that can cause grievous injury. It can probe, search, debate, inquire, reason, speculate or despair. It can conjecture, deliberate, deceive, imagine or aspire. It can do many things. It has brought man to the crossroads.

Man's mind is at a stupendous juncture. Either it destroys everything there is, or moves on to something beyond, beyond mind.

Maybe we await a mind totally at peace with itself, with no contradictions and no conflict. We await a mind peaceful like a very still sea, powerful, always in a state of quiet readiness, a mind pristine and pure. A mind that observes every ripple, every glimmer; even the microscopic does not elude it. It is sensitive, deeply sensitive, but silent at its core. In that deep silence, is perhaps a possibility not envisaged before.

Is such a silence possible in this increasingly noise-filled world? Perhaps just one man's silence is enough, just one whose silence is truly silence. Imagine the repercussions of that silence. The repercussions of a Buddha are still being felt. His peace still touches each heart that comes in contact with it—a golden silence, a golden contagion that awaits its appointed hour.

A Divine Canvas

Can a page remain blank? Can a day be totally uneventful, totally vacant, erased out of our memory? This day is like a fresh canvas, ready to record its happenings. It invites a fresh picture to be painted. We must bring in the ingredients to give shape to this picture. Life relies on us to bring in the raw materials and effort. It gives us an ideal or goal to work towards. Problems and pitfalls may come along the way, but the goal beckons. We must achieve our goal for the picture to reach completion. Life stands back as witness to its own goals being completed.

Photo: Pradeep Malhotra

We are full of anxiety on seeing a blank new canvas. What on earth are we going to draw or paint? Where are we to start? Where is our inspiration? Who will guide us on the way? What if the paint runs out? What if my ideas run dry? What if I produce a horrible caricature which will make me a laughing stock? The mind is a whirlwind of conflicting emotions, stable one moment, in deep crisis in the next. Where lies the mind's escape? Do I go this way or that?

. I decide I will go this way. And the way leads into a path that becomes a road to my destination. Once we have decided upon a goal, the path itself opens up, circumventing detours and blockages in its way. I see this happening each time I take a firm decision. A much-desired trip to the Kumbh Mela materialises right in front of my surprised eyes despite the many obstacles in my way. I could take a trip in the company of like-minded people who too were on inward journeys. It was as if the Divine answered 'I have heard your call, you will come and see my face, in the faces of the thousands who come together'.

All true and sincere calls are responded to by the Divine. Our prayers and calls must match the frequencies of truth, peace, harmony, compassion and forgiveness. But how do we retain these frequencies as our constant companions in the face of the irritants of daily life, of noise, disharmony and hatred. How do we remain focussed in their midst? By stilling our hearts? By being dispassionate in the face of disturbance and provocation, by overruling an aspect of ourselves?

Could we do it by transcending the dualities we face at every step, each the other side of the same coin, and seeing them in another light? By seeing them from another plane, where all life and myriad manifestations, evolving situations and possibilities are as one, coming from and going to the same source. Then, life takes on a new meaning. A new picture is painted on a blank canvas, a painting that is divine.

A Dynamic, Tranquil Repose

It is a cold wintry day. The foggy atmosphere seems to creep into my body. I have reinforced myself with a double layer of clothing. We need to feel warm. We need to feel protected and safe. We need home, family and most importantly, the feeling of being surrounded and supported by the Divine. This cold day, my heart goes out to all who feel denied these vital needs. I feel a deep gratitude for what I have received, which I probably do not deserve.

But what is deserved and what is undeserved? The Divine gives unstintingly to all, its blessings are for each thing in existence. It is we who must be fit to receive it. Receiving a gift is no simple thing. We must be prepared to receive; our hearts must be open to receive. Can we imagine being given gifts while our hands are closed tight? Give and receive with open hands, open hearts and open minds.

We look at the earth and its abundance, given openly and freely: land, air, water, forests, flowers…the list is endless. What is expected of us in return? Just to be in harmony with the seasons, the cycles, with reverence for the divine plan. All we need is to be in harmony with ourselves.

What is my role in the face of this great global disharmony that surrounds us? My role is to be in harmony with myself even in the face of aggravating circumstances. I only need to be true to myself. I accept the truth in things, not superficial falsehoods. Every situation has its underlying truth. The situation may be surrounded by falsehood but underlying it is a greater truth. It is this greater truth which is my goal. It is this truth that I must see in all things and beings, a truth that transcends time and space.

Could it be that we are here to transcend our earthly limitations, on earth but not of the earth, divine beings, undertaking an earthly journey with a divine purpose? We are instrumental 'beings'. We have not just to do but also to be. And we must be 'that,' live in a memory of 'that,' in a dynamic remembrance. Each moment and in all things, we must be instruments of a divine will that manifests in peace and silence.

A Moment When Man Decides

Indomitable wills, unwavering courage, we see these in the lives of the great. Where do they get their strength? Where do they get their courage? What is their motivating force? These are some thoughts and questions that come to mind when looking at the lives of Mahatma Gandhi, Sri Aurobindo and Rabindranath Tagore, great men and sages from our very recent past.

Photo: Pradeep Malhotra

We have no doubt they have been in the presence of the Divine. Their lives have been transformed by a divine force. The Divine has found in them a receptive channel, ready to obey the command, ready to take the plunge. Have they have bypassed the ordinary methods of going through deep penetrating study, debate, books and all the other normal methods? Perhaps, these too, but most importantly, they have imbibed from the source, through a process of osmosis and direct contact. They have come in contact with the divine fire while searching and have been consumed by it: *'lalli dekhan main gayee, main bhi ho gayi lal'* as the poet Kabir put it.

Their aspiration has matched that of the flame, intense and unrelenting. They have aspired for only 'that' and 'that' has responded to the call, like magnets attracting each other. So too must our aspiration be, pointed, like an arrow speeding to its destination. The target beckons and our aim must be straight and unwavering. Our lives need to be unwavering in the light of the truth discerned. The light may be hazy, but with time it becomes increasingly clear. The veil of illusion and deception is torn and its tricks and charades are exposed.

A silent mind can discern with clarity the many forces at play, not tricked into accepting every trick they play. These forces are there at each moment, in varying hues and intensities. Our job is to see through them. Beyond all deceptions is a divine singular truth of which we are children. All creation is a crystallisation from this one source.

We are living in a time when the forces of this deception are reaching a peak, waiting for us to succumb. It is also a time when the conscious force of the Divine is waiting to claim its supreme victory. It is a moment when man decides whether he is to exceed himself or to remain in delusion forever, to close a chapter before it has a chance to open its first page. We are at that hour that Sri Aurobindo has called 'the hour of God,' an hour when we take a supreme leap of faith and cross over to the realm of truth and divinity which is our inalienable right and inheritance.

A New Birthday for Humanity?

It is my brother's birthday today. How time has flown! We were children just yesterday, celebrating our birthdays in the company of our parents. Today, they are no longer here. How things change; truly, nothing is forever. Everything has a beginning, middle and an end, as my mother pointed out to me just before her passing. She wanted me to understand this fundamental truth and be strong. When I examine this statement closely, I realise that it applies to everything. Things start as ideas, small tentative beginnings gather momentum and strength, reach a transitional equilibrium and then peak. And then begins a reverse cycle, hastening things to their inevitable ends, either gradually or abruptly. It is a cycle no one and nothing can escape. It is God's will, the way things are ordained.

The Lord's Prayer says 'Thy will be done'. The divine will is all encompassing, all knowing and all wise. It has factored in all measure of things. All permutations and combinations have been taken into account. Every detail is worked out. We need to be in harmony with God's plan and not keep rushing at all moments with arbitrary solutions and fixes we have in mind. Each of our 'solutions' is in conflict with millions of 'solutions' being imposed by others; none are in harmony with the divine plan.

We need to be silent, to hear, by deep intuition, God's plan. In our silent moments, we have, time and again, intimations of truth and the right course of action. We need to trust our deepest intuition and go forward. Our deepest spiritual insights are through our intuition. Perhaps, a deeply spiritual life is a deeply intuitive life. The word intuition itself is instructive: 'in-tuition' or a teaching from within. It is for this reason we are told that 'the kingdom of God lies within'. It is in vain that we search for this kingdom outside of us, in things, pleasures, power and relationships. In silence, we realise that we are kings of a vast empire, the riches of which are yet to be explored. Is the age of external exploration over and has a new adventure begun?

'An adventure of consciousness' is how Sri Aurobindo and the Mother describe the next leg of man's evolution. The next revolution is further evolution, accelerated evolution. The past is gone; it is obsolete. It has played its necessary part, but now that chapter is closed. We are on to a paradigm shift.

Could it be for this reason that the old solutions no longer work? The context has changed. The map of the world has changed; it remains the same only superficially. There has been a revolution in the earth's atmosphere. A gestating cocoon is ripe and ready to burst, but the earth's new birth is being delayed by each of us. We are afraid and confused. All our certainties are at a dead end. We are not sure what this gigantic confusion is leading up to—this gigantic clash of wills and this enormous technological wave. Will this cocoon release a monster? Is it a harbinger of global disaster? Or is it a nebulous, mysterious preparation to release a beautiful butterfly, a new consciousness announcing a fresh new birthday for humanity?

A Tranquil Fire at the Heart of Things

Why do we expect something concrete each day, some fixed result, something very tangible like money, material goods or even relationships? We want results all the time. Study, effort, exam and result! It just goes on. What is my concrete expectation of today? Can it be defined, quantified? The mind wants something to chew on; it can't keep still. So, what do I do today? Let me see my check list, my diary, my 'to do' list.

Photo: Pradeep Malhotra

Is this way of being a must, the only way? Must we always be thinking or doing? To always be thinking, 'what next'? Or what happened yesterday or what will happen tomorrow? If I don't do something, what will happen? I am in a panic. I must do something. Doing nothing is not an option. Just being is not an option. Or maybe it is, just being present in the moment, to the moment and being fully alive in this moment. To savour this moment wholly and completely, without thought about the past or the future or of doing something with it or to it. When nothing needs to be done, I will do nothing, and I will be perfectly ready when something needs to be done. I am perfectly self-contained doing nothing at all, just living in the moment. Just being as the moment wants me to be…just being.

Like a lotus in the pond, I am content to be, not concerned if I am seen or appreciated. I am content to live one day or a hundred. I live in the eyes of a divine witness, a silent witness who sees all with equal eyes. Who has seen ages come and go with equal eyes—kingdoms, empires, battles, birth, death, cataclysm, deluge, destruction, reconstruction, annihilation and rebirth. None is great, none is small. All things are seen through a tranquil gaze that understands and accepts all.

A tranquil fire is at the heart of all things, all hearts. It is a fire burning in all things in existence. It is a silent fire that we may not even see. It is a fire that unites all, the bird to the tree, the tree to the man, the man to earth, the earth to the oceans, the oceans to the sky and the sky to the cosmos. It connects the cosmos to existence, to consciousness.

It is a fire at the heart of consciousness. Suddenly, we are becoming conscious of ourselves. We are becoming conscious of who we really are. We are waking up from our long sleep. We are waking up to ourselves.

Ambushed by Silence?

Rapid, unprecedented change! What am I to do in this situation of ever-changing circumstances and change? What is that part of me that is ever stable and peaceful in the middle of this perplexing flux? In the midst of earth-shaking happenings and strife, can I remain unaffected? Perhaps, it is for the first time that I feel part of a global whole and feel the aftershocks of what is happening in remote corners of the world.

The rapidity of developments is stunning, mind boggling. I feel like I have been hit by a sledgehammer. I do not know what to expect next. I am in flux, in limbo. The transition has caught me unawares and I react explosively. My mind is not at peace, my relationships uneasy. Uncertainty has made me edgy and distrustful, cynical…even suicidal.

I want nothing to change, especially in relation to myself. I want deference from all to my demands, my irrevocable positions. I have an opinion on others' opinions. Everything is me and mine! Is this clash and clamour the end of everything I have known? Is this confusion an endless pressure for me to change? Bits and bytes of information at every step, cross communication, loud noises, and a babel of voices. Endless knowledge, but where is the wisdom? Where can I be heard in this volcano of noise and sound?

Where is this endless clamour leading to? I hear the unceasing sounds of car horns blaring, dogs barking, the tring-ring of cycle bells, engines revving, the sudden screech of brakes, buses racing and children crying out to their mothers. I see the sameness of it all every day—things rapidly changing yet nothing really changing at all. RIP— died of a massive stroke of boredom or of sudden, rapid change which brought no change. Will things ever really change? When will this clamour end?

Is God listening? How could he possibly be, with all this noise and rush? Perhaps, he waits for things to slow down a bit, for things to become a bit quieter.

As I slow down, I might be able to hear what the next person is trying to say. I will listen to him with full attention. All these years, he has been trying to get someone to just listen to him. Can I hear him out?

And yes, God, I will be silent. I will listen to you in the silence of my heart. It is there that you speak wordlessly. You are always there waiting and ready to ambush at a moment's notice. And in that silence, I am ready to be ambushed.

Consciousness is Just a Call Away

May each being be consciously enveloped in the Divine. That is a comforting thought, as comforting as a snug, warm blanket. A feeling of being loved and wanted, protected against all dangers. All beings need this protection, need to feel the divine presence.

A society that feels protected is carefree. Each person at his most creative, doing what comes to him best, dedicating his mind and energies to a self-chosen task consecrated to the Divine. Each person is a manifestation of the Divine and so, unique. Let us help in the flowering of this uniqueness. This same person will not come this way again.

Photo: Pradeep Malhotra

Let each person find his unique talents, his divine inspiration. Let each person's life flow in harmony with the divine will. Let it become an offering to the eternal, an offering from the sincerity of one's heart. Let it be an offering of aspiration, love, tears and flowers, of one's very being. Imagine all creation offering its very being to the Divine—an earth being transformed in some image of heaven. Imagine a golden age unfurling itself in front of our eyes.

In deep silence, divinity touches divinity, for all is divine. Can anything be other than divine, if everything comes from one divine source? A self-correction must take place in our vision. Our 'I' centred vision must give way to one that is multi-dimensional and all-encompassing, where all things are embraced in their totality. We are no longer objects or playthings of forces and events. We are integral and whole, part of a divine consciousness.

This consciousness is asking us to become aware of ourselves, to know who we really are. We ourselves are that consciousness. We are a consciousness aware of itself, no longer splintered and uncertain. The trials and pangs of our past were an essential stimulus to our evolving awareness. Each upheaval has incrementally brought us to a new threshold. The present cataclysmic events herald a fresh new breakthrough.

Our mental consciousness is being churned to frenzy. All that is gross, negative and evil should be drained out, leaving only a pure consciousness intact. Perhaps this churning may be a necessary evil, if only to save the patient from himself. The patient may be in ICU, but God says, 'Be brave, I see you. The saving light of consciousness is just a call away.'

Evolution's Pressure Cooker is Bursting

A feeling of being needed, wanted—why is this a fundamental need? Why is it so essential, so critical, to our existence? We are surrounded by things and objects that exist without consciously knowing whether they are needed or not. They play their appointed roles and move on. There are no questions asked or answers given. Why must we wallow in our misery?

Is it importance that we seek? Do we crave recognition? Do our egos take a big hit when we do not get the importance we think we deserve? Are we born with this flaw? Even a child wants recognition. Or are we missing the big picture? Does the child seek assurance, a feeling of being one with its surroundings, its family, its playmates, not alienated, not separated? Perhaps, each of us wants to be one with all that surrounds us, to be one with creation. We want no separation whatsoever. We want to embrace all things within our humanity. At the core, intuitively, we know all is one and that there is no other. We are part and parcel of one fabric. Destroy a part and all is destroyed.

Our deepest longings are those of being united with the Divine. We seek the Divine in all that surrounds us. We know that we are part of that divinity. Perhaps, it is as 'divine beings' that we look at our inner selves. Our dreams are of heaven and bliss right here on earth. Perhaps, we are divine beings transplanted in human form, to bring a divine consciousness to this planet.

God wants to be conscious everywhere. He plays this game of hide and seek, in minerals, in plants, in animals and in man. He prepares to reveal himself. But he awaits our consent and collaboration. He is a democrat. He is democracy personified. He will reveal himself when everyone is ready. He is preparing everyone for this moment. We too must play our parts, be ready for the moment. We must let go of all fear, all hesitancy, and all confusion. It is not a collapse we are headed towards, or a civilisational Armageddon. Contrary to all appearances, it may be the advent of another consciousness, something radically new…a consciousness so new that we are unable to recognise its form. We see faint glimpses in moments of intuition; these vanish as soon as we try to hold on. A mischievous elf—now you see it, now you don't—this consciousness says there is no way you can trap me.

We have got into the habit of trapping things and keeping them under our control as evident from the vast galleys of slaves in our factories, schools and offices. But the slave is now revolting; he has had enough. The pressure cooker is bursting. Evolution was the pressure cooker and evolution is also the release. Accelerated evolution! Our goose is cooked… could it be a tasty dish is on its way?

Flying Blind...or Coming Home?

One prays: 'May the Divine hold all in its embrace. May no being feel unloved or unwanted. May all consciously know that they live in a divine presence. May they always be aware of the blessings surrounding them. May all lives become the life divine.' That is the prayer that goes out from our hearts today, a prayer that has been on the lips of mankind from ages past, a prayer that asks the Divine to reunite man with itself. This separation has gone on for too long. It has reached a breaking point, a juncture reached where a total annihilation of mankind is a possibility... also the possibility that mankind is once again re-united with its divine source.

Photo: Pradeep Malhotra

All the signs are here—catastrophic events, mind-boggling changes, cataclysms, rebellion, a loss of values, confusion, end-of-the-world and doomsday cults, everyone and everything is out for itself. A storm of storms is ripping the world apart, bringing all the fault-lines into the open. An old order has collapsed and a new order is yet to be born. A mayhem of the mind and ego, a carnival of the low and ugly, with all that needs to be thrown out masquerading as a saviour. A churning is in process. All that needs to be rejected is being propelled to the very top. Is this churning holding back a new consciousness that wants to emerge? This froth, a last vestige of an old decaying order, how long will it be able to prevent the volcano of a new consciousness from erupting?

What is this new consciousness? How does it want to manifest? How does it undermine an old order? It is a silent consciousness. Perhaps it achieves its ends in silence. Its heart lies in the creative process, in creation itself—the divine will manifest as consciousness. It is consciousness that is everywhere. Every little thing is imbued with it. Every little thing is awakening to it. We have been un-conscious for too long. We open our eyes in wonder. We see it in the smallest of things and then we don't. Someone or something is playing hide-and-seek with us. It wants us to seek, to find. The moment we think we have something in our grasp, it vanishes.

What are we to make of this? What is someone or something trying to tell us? We were in search of something and now someone is giving us the clues. We had implored the divine to reunite us with it, our source. Today, we are being shown a path, glimpses of light that suddenly come, and then, just as suddenly, disappear. We are flying blind in a thick fog when suddenly there is the faint glimmer of the runway lights. Could we be coming home, where we always belonged?

Honey Bees in Search of Gold

What will this day bring in its wake, I wonder. Each day is brand new with all the promise of everything fresh and unexplored. It is an invitation and a promise to new delights and experience.

We are always in search of the new, things that we have not seen or done before. At heart, we remain adventurers, ever ready for the next mystery…and the next. Is the universe a mystery waiting to be constantly explored? Is there treasure waiting for us at every step? Perhaps there is, and we just don't know. Perhaps, we need fresh new eyes to see each day, eyes that are not clouded by the colours of the past. The past is gone and the future is yet to be. What we have is the present, open to possibility. Everything in the present is a possibility, a mysterious box waiting to be opened.

We need to be curious but we must wait silently for what is to come. Whatever comes, we are happy. We do not want to hold on to this treasure or happy moment forever, for the next moment brings yet more riches and happiness. Our happiness relies on what we release. The more we release, the more we enjoy the freedom to savour the next moment. We are honey bees, releasing our nectar before our next foray.

Our consciousness is a constant 'now,' evolving moment to moment, never still, never stagnant. It is a consciousness co-evolving with the cosmos, all creation part and parcel of its movement. We are one body, different aspects of the same body…the eyes, the heart and the limbs. The pain of one part is the pain of all, just as joy too is transmissible. 'I have become contagious,' the Mother said, speaking of a new consciousness now spreading.

Trying to come to terms with this nascent consciousness, the world today lurches from one side to the other precariously. What does the present clash and rumble forebode? Are we at some end-point, a point of no return? Has man's mind reached its culmination? Is man on his way out? Is he redundant, obsolete? Is he declared extinct? Or is it time for his 'outward' mind to turn 'inwards'? Perhaps, all those riches are not out there but right here. Perhaps, he does not realise how rich he is and that all his treasures lie in his consciousness.

Perhaps he is un-conscious at this moment. This is a wakeup call to connect the dots, to see the larger picture… to see where he, himself, fits in. It is a jigsaw. We see a faint and nebulous something but many vital pieces are yet missing. Someone is playing a game. We are part of that game. Is our greater consciousness playing a game of hide-and-seek, a game where it seeks and we hide, a game where it hides and we seek?

In Peace and Silence, the Eternal Manifests

Everything is so fragile. Just last evening, I saw this moth buzzing around my table; today, it lies lifeless. How fragile its life was! Yet, it lived its brief span, a part of that noticed by me. Today, I have blown it off my desk with just one small breath. Our every thought, every emotion, every action is fragile. Together, these little, fragile moments make a whole, long life: '*Chahey thodi bhi ho, yeh umar badi hoti hai…*' the old haunting melody goes.

Photo: Pradeep Malhotra

Can we imbibe, in these brief moments, a deep love that we sense resonating across the universe? After our life journeys are over and we are gone, what is left? Only the faint footprints and the resonances we leave behind. The Buddha, Mahavira, Christ, their resonances are still in the air. So, when I go, what will my reverberances be? Of peace, tranquillity, beauty, harmony, purity, brotherhood, serenity?

Of some living merger with the Divine? Of a life that is all this in thoughts, in actions, in waking moments and in sleep.

Can I live in remembrance from moment to moment, never forgetting that all life is a movement towards a union with the Divine? That even the worst of circumstances is a manifestation of the Divine, a temporarily darkened movement moving towards its inherent divinity, a movement from darkness to light?

Those thousands of little moments we have seen and experienced since we were born, where are they taking us? What did they mean? What do they mean? Are we in a progressive state of awakening from moment to moment? Are we being aroused from a deep slumber? Is evolution a progressive awakening? Is evolution a spiral with many transitional stages? Where does this divine consciousness want to take us?

Perhaps, this evolving consciousness wants all of us to be one with itself, to move as it does, with no fixed destination. Its light goes where it is needed most, where it has to be; it does what it has to do. It works, creates and acts in peace and silence, surrounded by peace and silence. We observe this present moment shorn of its noise, doubt, anguish, insecurity and uncertainty, in its purity. We see this present moment surrounded by eternity, as an eternal moment with no beginning and no end. We see just this moment, with no expectation from the past or future…just peace, just silence.

'In peace and silence, the eternal manifests.'

Is Consciousness Saying Something?

A deep feeling that consciousness is trying to tell us something, that things are moving towards some culmination, yet also towards some new beginning. The things that are happening are hidden from the eyes of man. Each thing, each event on earth, is moving as if in some hidden stream, a stream of consciousness on the move. There is a feeling that every thing is being pushed, or even pulled, towards where it should rightfully be, a co-arising, a co-evolution, with every single being brought to an inner harmony and nothing less.

It is as if creation is saying I have created all things in my own light, equal. Now, the time has come for all differences to disappear, to dissolve. The time has come for all things to be conscious of who they really are. All things are 'me' in my glory. All things must awake; the time for their evolutionary sleep is over. That sleep was but a gestation, a transition for a miracle to brew, like a butterfly in the making in the womb of a cocoon. That long, dark night is soon to be over.

Is man prepared for this great transition? He feels a great change coming. He feels it in his bones. He is apprehensive, uncertain, terrified. He does not know what is coming in its wake. He was happy till late, about the way things were. Perhaps, not happy, but accepting of whatever was. He knew his place in the scheme of things. Or did he? Today, the ground below his feet is disappearing. All his certainties, his foundations, are crumbling. A deep, long rumble is heard. Is that the *tandava* of Shiva's dance, heralding death and destruction? Or is it a thunderous call, heralding the arrival of something brand new, something unexpected? A clarion call to man, to be up, to be alert or to miss the moment, which is a rare moment that comes once in thousands of years.

This moment does not care for our mental constructs and certainties, or our technological achievements or our visions of an economic paradise. It does not care for our philosophies and theories. It does not care for our house of cards. It cares only for one thing, that one pure note that comes from the core of our hearts, for that one cry, pure and unstained, from the depths of our soul. Only for that one aspiration pure and straight, an aspiration and consecration that goes straight towards the supreme divine.

Navigating through the mist of life

Today is an overcast day, with a forecast of rain. There is some bad weather ahead. I hope it will get better before we set out on our journey, otherwise this just might turn out to be a hazardous, unpleasant venture.

We are always hoping for things to happen our way, while there are many imponderables en route. Life has an uncertain quality to it. While driving through a heavy storm, fog and mist, all our normal signposts could be obliterated and we might have to rely on anticipating hurdles and a bit of luck and a prayer. Life is a question mark; our greatest certainties are open to question.

Photo: Pradeep Malhotra

How do we navigate through this maze? One wrong step and you are swallowed by a great marsh pit. With some effort, you are left just floundering. I wonder if there is a better way of going about. The road of competition saps the life out of us. A life purely of the intellect dries us out. A life only of action may not fit the bill. We are left questioning the meaning of it all. Yet, despite all the questioning and imponderables, life must be lived each day, each moment. Life should be filled with meaning, each day.

Can this great cosmos, this great creation be without meaning? Each thing, even the littlest, is governed by some greater law, imbued with meaning and purpose. Some of this meaning is apparent and some not so, hidden from sight till the time is right. We need to prepare ourselves to see all things in perspective. Perspective in place, all things fall into order, from the smallest to the biggest. The mind no longer dissects and analyses. It no longer adds up and weighs. It no longer reduces things to their components. It sees the larger picture; it sees its own role in a larger picture. It is a whole picture that is evolving. It is consciousness in motion and we are part of that consciousness.

Where does this consciousness want us to go? What road does it want us to take? This consciousness is pointing us in a direction. It seems to say that we are not puppets unsure of our destiny. We are active participants in our own evolution. Man is in the process of exceeding himself. He is not final. He is in pursuit of his essence, that which links him to the Divine. His destiny is in the process of manifesting. There are many difficulties along the way. The Divine is trying us on a touchstone. Can divinity be a prize for the weak? Here is the greatest prize of them all, all that humankind has hoped and prayed for since its creation—the erasing of the barrier between man and God.

Nurturing the Flower Within

Our eyes and sensations are always fixed on the external world. We have very little time to nurture our real self to its harmonious potential. We find ourselves embattled in this world of pressures and demands. Our waking moments are spent in an irritable doing of things against our volition. A constant abrasive quality is in the air, a kind of corrosion that does not let us live in peace for long. It is a battering that goes on relentlessly. Each day, things that we value most, break down. It remains a losing battle.

In this unremitting onslaught, where is the time to nurture our real self, to give it the warmth, love and encouragement it so desperately needs? The child in us requires constant support till it is ready to stand on its own. Any neglect and it wilts, and repeated neglect may just kill it, never to resurface. Can we learn to be gentle with ourselves? Not recriminating, not blaming and not forever delving into some sorry past. The past is gone and the future is still to come.

An acceptance of ourselves and our strengths and weaknesses is the first step. We take a grand overview of ourselves in the larger scheme of things. Just as the Divine loves all equally, so must we. And I must love myself equally, fully accept myself, and not compare myself with anyone. There is only one me. I am unique. There was never one like me and there will never be. There must be a method in the Divine's doing. He creates unique individuals, not duplicates.

Our criticism of ourselves comes when we compare ourselves with others. We compare qualifications, possessions and opportunities, not realising that everyone is unique, born into different circumstances and with different abilities and different possibilities. And then we say, 'let a million flowers bloom and bring in their wake a million fragrances'.

Our life too needs to become a fragrance, an offering to the Divine, a unique fragrance lovingly nurtured to produce an exquisite note and make the world become a more fragrant place. The world could become more accepting in its presence with life's abrasive moments smoothened and its jagged edges blunted.

One sees this in the life of sages, those who have explored the depths of life, its highs and lows, who have been single pointed in their quest, who gave of themselves rather than took, who embraced all humanity. In the face of a rising storm, theirs was a blissful calm, even under grave provocation, a respectful silence, and a greater patience with the ills of the world and a self-giving collaboration with time.

Between the Lines, Behind The Shadows

Push one thing and two others move; they, in turn, push or move other things and a chain reaction goes on. We are each part of this chain, pulled sometimes and pushed sometimes, pulling sometimes and pushing sometimes. We are where we are because of these pulls and pushes. Evolution is the pusher; all that is involved, drawn in, is in the process of evolving.

In the midst of this pulling and pushing, the divine imperative takes us where it will. It knows its goal in the midst of millions of pulls and pushes. It nudges creation silently, through an ever-expanding consciousness that knows no bounds. This consciousness is always at a cutting edge and always on the brink of something more encompassing, ever widening and ever growing. All things submerged in this ocean of consciousness, its pliant tentacles grow vaster and vaster with each passing day.

Photo: Pradeep Malhotra

Man's consciousness is no longer restricted; it is to become one with the universe, equal with creation's original impulse. This is a throbbing, a rhythm, a melody taken up by all creation in harmony that is still falling into place. The presence of a coming new order, a new equation, is seen by man in his present state as disorder, a disruption of age-old, established laws. All creation is now in a state of dynamic disequilibrium, moving towards a newer centre and equilibrium, a disharmony moving towards a larger harmony. It is an original vibration at the heart of things moving towards its truer centre. Things that are hidden from our sights are moving towards a clearer picture; discordant notes are moving towards a greater agreement and harmony. Some great sweep, some great tide, takes mankind towards a new crest, some vast epiphany.

The intimations of a new world are everywhere. Suddenly, nothing is what it seems, only seemingly so. If only we could see between the lines, behind the shadows, amid the scenes.

The ordinary, the routine, holds it secret tight. This day like all days, this moment like all moments, does not reveal the truth it hides. This truth bides its time and will only reveal itself when its time has come. Till then, evolution plays its monotonous role, all things moving from preceding things. One step followed by the next and then the next, time following its honoured tradition.

But now a rapid evolutionary movement is seen, a hundred steps multiplied by ten and then, by hundred. A run, then a gallop…are we to transcend time? There are strange intimations in the air, nothing is the same anymore; this heart now beats to another drum and the drummer holds the key. Man is unhinged from his moorings; he is no longer man. Does he now move to another state? Like the first fish on land, he takes his first steps, tentative, uncertain. Where to next, he wonders.

Surrender

To surrender is to give ourselves up to a greater force, to give up totally and completely, relinquish our smaller identity, to acknowledge that we are in the presence of something more encompassing, more knowing, and something whole, of which we are an integral part.

In surrender, it is the 'I' that surrenders. It is the ego that surrenders. It realises that it does not know enough, does not have enough experience and cannot do enough. The 'I' or the intellect can go so far but no further. It can conceive brilliant philosophies, plan, build, construct machines and more. That is how far it can go. It cannot answer 'who am I' or 'why am I here'. It cannot answer the most crucial questions facing mankind. The 'I' comes to a dead end, draws a blank. Man's progress comes to a halt. He does not know where to look next, what to do next. A question mark faces his every step. Why is he doing what he is doing? Today, man is well and truly stumped. There is no going back, and going forward too is a question mark.

He has tried it all with every branch of knowledge at his disposal. Today, this very knowledge has brought him to his knees. He no longer knows how to harness this knowledge into a whole. Technology run amok is in control of him. With each new 'discovery,' he releases a bullet that ricochets and wounds him in the process. Every 'solution' is followed by failure or collapse. Where does he go from here? He has tried everything and nothing works. Nothing at all!

So, he now looks within, into his innermost recesses, into the silent parts of his being. There, in the womb of silence, he finds the answers needed. He does not know where these answers come from or even how they come. He feels an inner sense of certainty as to outcomes. He has surrendered his diehard ideas, opinions and intellect to a force higher than himself, a force all-knowing and wise, compassionate and understanding.

His surrender brings into his life a flow of unimaginable proportions, all-encompassing, fluid, harmonising and filled with love and peace. It asks no questions, expects no answers. It just flows, carrying all in its wake, enveloping all in its embrace. It is a mellow flame touching all with its light, enlightening the darkened corners of our beings. It lifts us from our pre-historic past to our conscious, enlightened future, our individual consciousness equal with consciousness itself. It helps man exceed himself, taking him towards the Divine.

Today, rather than the individual, the collective man is at this fortunate juncture. He must exceed himself. He must exceed himself if he is to keep his date with destiny. And for this, he should surrender what he is for what he is yet to be.

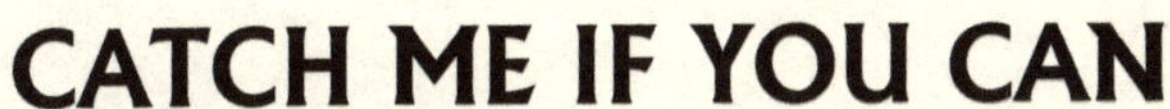

CATCH ME IF YOU CAN

A Chink, A Crack, An Opening

A chink, a crack, an opening, that is all that is required to unveil a mystery that is now very old. There is a time for mysteries and a time for the truth. Creation's bag is full to overflowing; it is bursting to tell its truth. How long will it do its endless rounds before its secret of secrets one day comes tumbling out?

Photo: Pradeep Malhotra

All creation is one. All things are one. We are one consciousness on an eternal journey. Today, we are growing conscious of this journey, with the creator and the creation on the same page, co-partners in this journey, co-evolvers. All beings are sounding boards to each other, each reflecting the other. We sense a crisscrossing of connections, one thing touching another, and we sense too, the unfolding of a divine consciousness hidden in man. It is Krishna's consciousness that cascades among the waves, shining amid the skies. It is Krishna witnessing his creation as himself and us witnessing Krishna as his many selves.

There is trepidation in my heart. Is Krishna himself telling me something? Is this disquiet actually Krishna bringing me to a greater awareness of a divine presence hidden everywhere? 'I manifest in all things simultaneously, the great and the small. I manifest unheard, unseen. I manifest in all things, in all creation. I manifest in life, in death. I manifest in thought, in silence. I manifest in the depths of the oceans, in the planets far and wide the eyes can't see. I was manifest then, and now…I manifest forever'.

'I am the dance of the atoms, of the molecules, of evolutionary plasma…a manifestation and a taking back, a constant coming and going; an expansion and a contraction…now seen, now invisible…a fluid permutation of an endless process, nothing gained, nothing ever lost. … all contained in an original seed gestating in the womb of time'. I sense Krishna in the beat of this heart, Krishna in this sigh, Krishna to the left, Krishna to the right, Krishna as the pen in my hand, Krishna as I write and Krishna as this written word.

A great veil is lifted and Krishna is all I see. I am but Krishna's shadow. Krishna is you and Krishna is me!

Life's Impromptu Moments

An unexpected phone call, an impromptu get-together over coffee, an enjoyable hour together. Life takes on another meaning when things happen spontaneously. Things glide smoothly with no pulls or pressures. We float as if on a cloud. We are in the moment.

What if life could run spontaneously from moment to moment? 'On the go' events and happenings with events taking their course, with no force or pressure. The day has its broad contours but beyond that, things take on a meandering quality. Remember days of old when the pressures of life were not that great, when we had the leisure to be ourselves? Slow work schedules, afternoon siestas, an easy-going camaraderie and fewer pressures to conform. Is this some figment of my imagination? Or is it perhaps a pointer to another way of looking at and doing things. A life unhurried, a paradise found! What have we lost in this frenzied pace of life? No time to reflect, to contemplate, to go with the flow of time.

Can we see how plants and animals live, how seasons change, how rivers flow, how buds open to become flowers, how bees sense flowering, how birds migrate, how animals nurse their young, how elephants bathe in streams, how kittens play, how trees give shade, how clouds release rain, how peacocks dance to woo, how birds call?

Slow down, just watch and see—you have the whole world on natural TV. Slow down and watch your heart beat to the sound of another drummer. His drum beats to another tune, a tune in harmony with an eternal symphony and orchestra. In that eternal moment, we too become that moment. We become that. All separation vanishes and we are one with creation. We live from moment to moment in a golden glow with consciousness touching consciousness.

Completing the Jigsaw

We are coming ever closer to an event of momentous proportions. The trouble is we do not know what this event is, how it is to come about and exactly when. We only sense it in our bones. We see evolution has picked up speed, things are transforming right before our surprised eyes. Things that held good for centuries are disappearing in a flash. We are shell shocked. What on earth is happening is the question on our lips. What exactly, or what 'inexactly,' if that helps us, is happening?

Photo: Pradeep Malhotra

Why has nature decided to speed up evolution? Why has it become impatient with its age-old methods? Was our past in any way a run up to our future? Does the Divine now want to manifest consciousness openly in all things? Is the time of the unconscious now over? Is it time for a makeover? Was the earth being made conscious bit by bit all the time? Was it a gradual progression, from mineral, plant, animal to man? And now, is this a movement towards super consciousness, towards a super-man?

Man has reached a stage where his present state deeply discomfits him; he wants to move forward to the next stage. All the old gods are dead, tucked safely into archival memories. We now seek the new, the god that lives in this living moment. What is God worth if he is not here and now, in this dynamic, living moment? Perhaps, it is a time when the living, throbbing god is emerging from the core of everything that lives, throbs and is here on earth right now.

We see a million mutinies breaking out: local protests, green movements, and womens movements, the youth, the dispossessed, everyone and everything in a state of mutiny. Each one knows and feels something is missing, something vital without which life is not worth living. All the missing pieces must be brought together. The jigsaw should be complete.

Each piece of the jigsaw is now becoming conscious of itself and of every other piece. Perhaps a linking of consciousness is taking place, 'a planeterisation of consciousness,' the planet itself becoming conscious on this journey of our individual and collective self to meet our universal and eternal self. It is a journey that progressively reveals itself with each step that we take. It is an adventure that beckons, an adventure and a mystery that reveals itself as we play the game the Divine wants us to.

Random and chance—Steps to a Higher Evolution?

Do random and chance events too have logic behind them? The thought intrigues. What is random and chance after all? Out of sequence, not in any coherent order, plucked out of the hat? Perhaps, random and chance may belong to another order, to another pattern yet unseen. We are so used to seeing things in order, in sequence, in patterns, that when we encounter something that does not fit the bill, we call it random, chance.

Often, it is a random thought that catches our imagination and gives us a new break. Could random be in any way connected to the intuitive or to the synchronous? Sometimes, it is at random that we pick up a book and just the right passage, appropriate to the moment, pops up. At times, we decide at random on a path and then we chance upon an old acquaintance with whom we have some urgent business.

Do we then start doing things at random? The mind says no, but it remains alert to the possibilities. Evolution too has had its fair share of random events. There are so many 'ifs' attached to man's progress, to other species that came and went into extinction, to this present moment where all of us are today. Random events have shaped history, changed geography and will go on shaping things as they will. While ordered events smooth the flow of life, it is random events that change destiny, that seem to play a great role in serving the progress and evolution of consciousness.

Random and chance may make up another order. Man is now sufficiently progressed to integrate the random into his consciousness. This will impart to his movements a new wholeness, a new vigour and vibrancy. He will realise that a higher consciousness guides him through the random to a path he needs to take. We are in the process of being led to a brand new, sacred geography. We only need to give our consent; our feet will do the rest.

It is an unravelling of an endless ball of wool. Then, there is a realisation: there is no beginning nor is there an end. It is one vast continuation, a consciousness filled with love where order and random are one and the same. Each serves the divine cause in its own way. As we integrate this knowledge into our lives, our progress too becomes smoother. We no longer see the random and chance as pitfalls but as another order, perhaps as steps to a higher evolution that is taking us straight into the arms of the Divine.

Freedom!

Freedom! We are born free, but are yet in chains. We want to be free but don't know how. Freedom is our birth right, but how do we exercise this right? Freedom has its own smell—ask someone in chains, in bondage, someone for whom freedom is just a dream. Over the ages, the cry has been for freedom from the tyrant, the dictator, a hated regime. Freedom is fundamental to man. Today, this freedom is in the jaws of a tyranny of the self, of unbridled wants and desires, an economic and technological serfdom. Man, trapped by the self, is in bondage to the self.

Photo: Pradeep Malhotra

And then we see birds fly in freedom, turning here, turning there, taking a sudden dive, a twist, a turn. We yearn for that freedom. The bird does not know it is free. It does not ask for freedom. It just is...it is free. Just like a puppy playing by itself, it just is. No questions are asked, no answers expected, body and mind live in the moment, free. When birds are released from captivity how do they fly?

They don't know where to go. They are free but freedom is not theirs, not yet.

Man is free, yet in chains. He does not know what freedom means. What or who does he look up to for his freedom? He can only live within his own innate nature. He must live by his own *swadharma,* his true nature, or he will be the slave of someone else. As long as we are unsure of ourselves, we live by the dictates of others: what they think, what they feel, how they act. We are not qualified to question their motivations. We look up to and lap up the crumbs of another's appreciation. Our life is dictated by others, their wants, their desires, their whims. We are victims, waiting to be sacrificed.

Yet, a point is reached when we say, 'No more! I will live by my own *swadharma,* my own innate nature, and no matter what'. That is the first step to freedom. Just as a lion lives within his *swadharma,* without compromise. He is what he is and he is accepted for what he is. Not what he should try to be. Imagine what he would be if he were trying to be a deer or an elephant!

Man's essential nature is free, divine. The moment he deviates from his divine moorings, his *swadharma,* his freedom, is in danger. Today, he has reached a stage of acute un-freedom. A cry of agony is being heard from every quarter, a cry of enormous suffering, a living hell. Perhaps, a purge is what is now acutely needed, a purge of the body, mind and soul of the earth, of which we are nodes and vibratory strands, each uniquely tuned, each a vital part of the grand orchestra, each now undergoing a transformation.

Is this painful purge a process of transformation? We are ingredients in the pot, so we do not know. The master chef has a dish up his sleeve, so who are we to complain. Are we a self-offering to the supreme deity? Perhaps we are an offering of the best in us to the supreme divine, an offering that takes us towards freedom, total freedom.

Is a Transformation Underway?

No one wants to listen to the other. Each one is enmeshed in their own wants, desires and worries. Why listen to and take on yet more? A blind eye and a deaf ear suit the purpose, so we walk the pathways of the world, unseeing, uncaring, oblivious to the cries of our fellow man, each grievously hurt in some way or the other.

Where does our own anger end? What is the way out? Do we slash our way through, maiming and blinding all on the way? Where does our cry begin? Where does it end? Where is the court of last appeal? Is it perhaps in a non-complaining acceptance of what is? The complaints box is already full and can't take more. Perhaps 'what can I do best under the circumstances' might be more appropriate; silently waiting in a peaceful attitude might achieve much more. Yet the underlying sadness of it all does not seem to leave. A silent rage at the unfairness of it all, a sense of victimhood, anger, hatred and a desire for an avenging god. I want justice and I want it now! In my anger, I am ready to burn and destroy.

Maybe, out of this fire something pure might still emerge, like fresh shoots and grass emerging out of the embers of a forest fire. The forest and the fire are gone, yet the seeds of a new forest are present. Is this new forest more trusting and greener than the last one?

Perhaps our life is structured for this: to exhaust present possibilities and to bring us to the next. The great wars in

Europe gave way to the Euro zone, a time of peace. And now the crisis in Europe! Crisis…resolution…crisis! We move on, life moves on. When we look back, we see how much we have moved. A silent evolution has taken place surreptitiously, very stealthily and before we know it, we stand transformed.

Is a big transformation underway, disguised and hidden under many cloaks? Are anger, hatred and burning desires too its myriad faces? Whatever reaches its peak gives way to its opposite pole. Will peace and bliss follow in its wake or perhaps a deeper understanding into the real nature of things, so that nothing perturbs us anymore? Will we become accepting of life as it is, not disturbed by its vicissitudes: 'accepting earth's happenings with an equal soul…and hear in all things God's steps, his unseen feet tread destiny's pathways'?

Our rage gives way to an accepting quiet, and in that quiet, a message creeps in. The purity and quality of the message depends on the quality of our silence, like the crystal quality of water when the mud and dust has settled. A tranquil state emerges, unblemished; untouched by external circumstances, at peace with itself and with a certainty fully in place, which says God will always be by my side.

Take Each Day as it Comes

Take each day as it comes, because it will come packaged as it will, with its own shape and contours. To accept what it brings is in our hands. Not only to accept it, but to creatively touch or shape its contours. The day may start smoothly or on a rough note but if our inner mind is prepared, it smoothens out the day's rough edges. It remains witness to all that is happening, observing: this person is angry, this child is crying, this traffic is endless, this noise is deafening. Will it help if I get angry, or cry or lament? This will not change the situation but may contribute to its further worsening. This becomes an endless, vicious circle.

Photo: Pradeep Malhotra

Silence is the break to this endless cycle of observing thousands of little things daily, things that are hard or brittle, happy or sad, and colourful, without taking on their characteristics. This mind soundlessly softens the rough edges, smoothens and harmonises all events of the day.

We witness the image of the Buddha, silent and serene, emanating peace and bliss to the world. The Buddha lived some millennia ago but his silence, his harmony and bliss penetrate to this day. One man's victory over himself is a victory for all mankind; one man's perfection can yet save the world, as Sri Aurobindo said.

'In peace and silence the eternal manifests…allow nothing to disturb you and the eternal will manifest,' said the Mother. So simply put, yet so difficult for the human mind to comprehend and act on. The mind yearns to go in every direction. It is uncertain, unhappy and seeking an urgent answer to its situations and circumstances. A fundamental crisis is being faced by man, yet no answer seems forthcoming. The answer being sought is one that satisfies the needs of every being on this planet, a universal answer. Why is nature taking its time to give its answer? Nature may have millions of years at its disposal but does man have this luxury? He has to pack in a lot in the short span that he has been allotted. He has also to unpack and discard much that is obsolete.

Is anything small or unimportant? The small, the little, the microscopic is a building block of the universe. Without this small building block, we fall. See how each thing is pulling, or pushing the other? Everything is interconnected, every thing. We are one consciousness, small yet vital, interconnected parts of one universal consciousness. A co-arising is taking place, as the Buddha pointed. We are all in it together. Movements are now erupting globally; a universal aspiration is rising, an all-encompassing crisis is taking us steadily towards some newer consciousness and harmony.

A New World Waiting
to be Born

'If you want the world to be happy, first be happy in your own heart' says the Mother. That is so true, for if we are unhappy, how can the world be happy? Just as the pleasant smell of incense smoke touches all passers-by, so too will our happiness touch all those who come in contact with us. A smile brings out another smile and loving vibrations ripple all over.

If the world is seen as divine, all things become divine. All jarring and negative happenings too are seen in a divine light. As our thinking changes, so does the world. We witness this in the lives of our great teachers and *yogis*. The spark of their lives… that spark of oneness and divinity changed all who passed their way. One loving embrace is all it takes to bring home even the totally alienated, but our love needs to be whole and complete, like an all-giving shining sun that gently prises open the flower from the bud and the rain from the clouds.

Life is yoga, from the first to the last. It is silent yoga, a yoga of perfection. It is yoga for the Divine by the Divine. It is yoga for the joining of earth to heaven, the material to the non-material. It is yoga to discover, step by step, our eternal origins and our eternal destination. All else is a dalliance on the way, a brief sojourn, a coffee break; once this break is over, we are at the command of the Divine.

The Divine's gentle commands come to us through our hearts, impelling us to actions that help further evolution's hidden imperative. We are but its instruments, vibrating nodules of a vaster consciousness. We have so far been barely conscious. Now, evolution is taking its giant strides and asking us to be its active collaborators in its divine mission. It is asking us to join in an adventure of consciousness, an adventure of adventures. It is asking us to be strong. It is asking us to be ready. It is asking us to be conscious of this precious moment and not waste or misuse it. It is a moment that comes but once in millennia, an opportunity of a lifetime, perhaps one in many lifetimes.

Evolution wants us to have full trust in ourselves and in what this new consciousness brings. With this trust, it wants us to go forward. With each step that we take, we will be helped; our steps themselves will show us the way to a new world waiting to be born.

A Silence Full of Possibility

'May all separation end'… Perhaps mankind's sorrows have been caused by a pervasive feeling of separation from our source. We have lost an age-old sense of our origins: where we have come from and where we are going. We are alienated from our own selves. This feeling has separated man from man, and man from nature and his surroundings. He sees all things as separate entities. His sense of unity is gone.

Photo: Pradeep Malhotra

How is he to reclaim this unity, to break this separation, to reunite with all creation? This is the foremost question facing mankind. Will he be able to do this with a mental effort? Or does he need help from another source to pull him out of this predicament? The mind can go only so far and no further. While the mind can create structures of all kinds, with the slightest turbulence, these structures come tumbling down. Kingdoms and empires have come and gone, toppled and humbled by time. All around us lie the debris of these mind- and time-bound empires, raw materials and stepping stones to move in a radically new direction.

Could it be time to take a U-turn, to look into the divine within and to nature to provide us the answers? Can we silence our minds and give this creative stillness a chance? The answers may not satisfy our egos but may be in harmony with an eternal will. It is only in deep silence that we can hear what the eternal wills. We start to silence the incessant chatter of our minds. We start to silence our wants and desires. We start to silence the pulls and pressures of our bodies. Bit by bit, we silence all parts of our being. 'In peace and silence the eternal manifests…allow nothing to disturb you, and the eternal will manifest'.

Can anything at all manifest in a disturbed state? The whole of evolution has happened in a backdrop of peace and silence. The creation of planets, this cosmos, it all came about in the backdrop of a silence pregnant with possibility. Today, another possibility looms on the horizon, a possibility that wants to surpass all that has been done in the past. It wants to exceed itself. For that, it needs our active collaboration. We should be one with this possibility that has been man's deepest and age-old quest, his prayer and entreaty to the eternal to end all separation, to make man one with the Divine. Today, this possibility looms large on the horizon!

Travel Light in Body, Mind and Soul

The maintenance men have removed a cement cover and will now retrieve the water pump for cleaning and repairs. All systems work for a while and then with time, wear and tear and corrosion, they break down and collapse. Constant vigil and maintenance is a must if things are not to break down, but run smoothly.

So too, in our lives, we must remain in a state of all-round, body, mind and soul, well-being. One thing out of alignment leads to the whole system reaching a physical, emotional or spiritual collapse. Much like a machine, our physical, emotional and spiritual body too is a system linked to vaster systems like the family, community, country and planet, with each playing a vital part in our well-being.

This knowledge should be assimilated at an early age. This will prevent many a shock and surprise. Life will not be seen through the eyes of pain and revulsion at each unexpected turn and happening, which are, in reality, causally inter-linked. Inner wisdom at the very earliest is the greatest gift we can give to our young.

Increasingly, I see that the circumstances of my life have been organised to keep opening my eyes to new possibilities. Happenings and circumstances have made me sensitive. My life seems to have become a seismograph, minutely and acutely recording each little thing as it takes place, like the quivering of a budding leaf in the slightest of breezes, with the feeling deeply accentuated during moments of sorrow and grief.

Perhaps, we mirror our earth body going through a cataclysm. We are being made conscious of each part of its body: its forests, its seas, its deserts, its human and animal life, its seasons and cycles. Its symbiotic interrelationships and its co-arising can be clearly seen and felt. Every thing is interrelated. All consciousness is one. Your pain is my pain. I cannot be saved alone. Either all are saved or none at all. The choice is ours.

This phenomenon is being seen all over the globe, a co-evolution of ideas and thinking. It is a global link-up, with consciousness touching consciousness, light touching light and enlightening all. We unburden, too, the load that we have been carrying for long—all that is redundant, obsolete and to be given up. This is a new age, a new consciousness, calling. Be light, travel light in body, mind and soul!

Please Wait, You Are In Queue

Endless lines stretching interminably—queues. How are we so averse to them? Why is it that lines and queues irritate us and make us restless? Is it the spectre of endless boredom, the feeling of being static, rooted to a spot for eternity, that makes us feel so? One look at the long queue for the Aadhar card has sent me scampering home, to recharge over a cup of tea before I venture out again. Ah! That feels much better.

Photo: Pradeep Malhotra

Man is not a static being; he is always on the move. Even in sleep, his mind is on the move. Even while sitting in a spot, his mind is elsewhere. To be static and stationary is like a death sentence. Ask anyone incarcerated in an unwanted place or situation what he would not give for freedom to move at will, totally unhampered. Yet time and again, we have to stand in queues for something or the other. You make a telephone inquiry, only to be told you are in queue and will be attended to shortly; you are in queue at banks, municipal offices, railway stations, bill payment counters…you name it.

It seems half our lives are spent in queues. Is there a lesson in all these queues? I am sure there must be or God would have banished them a long time ago. Perhaps, queues are something we have not yet outlived. They are still part of an evolution we are going through. They are there perhaps to teach us patience for the larger lessons life has in store for us. Life is a process, always in a state of arriving, never having arrived. Life is a journey from one state to another; with the arrival of one state begins the journey to another. Queues are but brief halts in this journey.

Can we make the best use of these brief but seemingly interminable spaces? Perhaps, use them as a time to silence ourselves, to become quiet even, in the face of something alien to our natures. Can we go within, even while surrounded by many others also there on their currently agitated journeys? Each wants to be out of this seemingly endless wait at the earliest.

At its core is the word 'seemingly,' for what seems may perhaps not be the reality. What the queue gifts us and is preparing us for, is not for our eyes to yet see, not in our present state for sure. We make a small change in vision and take a detour. We look at our travail with equanimity. We look at the queue and our fellow travellers with sympathy and kindness. We look at ourselves too with kindness and in silence. From that compassion, that silence, something new might yet emerge, something that brews deep in the heart of compassion and silence.

A Little Golden Speck

To see the play of the Divine in all situations is yoga. Each day, with its many problems and pitfalls, becomes sublime with an overarching vision. The Divine Krishna sees through the minutest of things, all aspects of things, their past, present and future. He is in all things. He is all things—this ink, this pen, this hand, this thought. It is he who thinks, he who writes. Everything is done through him. He is the wood, the fire and the sacrifice. He is the one performing the sacrifice. The world, its beings and its happenings are integral parts of this sacred ritual. All that is, is sacred—each thing, each thought, each act.

If all is sacred, where do we stand today? We are in a state of unpreparedness, living in a past, whose expiry date is long gone! We are at a crossroads. We should move forward and take a vast leap into the future. In an act of great faith, we must offer ourselves to the sacrificial fire. It is a test of tests, with mankind being put to the test. We need to qualify for the new world in the making. We must be ready for what is to come.

The Divine has set the next stage of evolution. What evolution covered earlier over billions of years it now wants to do in a fraction of that time. Evolution has accelerated; God has stepped on the accelerator. A time has come to leave all preconceived ideas and notions behind. It is the hour of the unexpected.

The signs are here: a new wave has hit the earth. Each creature feels it in his bones. The old order is crumbling, preparing for an exit. What of the new? It is still trying to make its presence felt. We can feel its tentative vibrations if we are very observant and sensitive to its harmonies. We cannot pinpoint or hold these down. The new vibrations will not be held captive by old religious scriptures or by mental effort. In fact, there seems to be a ripple of laughter if you try to do so. All traps are child's play for it. These vibrations are more like a warm golden presence that sees all, accepts all and comforts all. It wraps all creation in its warm gentle cocoon, the womb of eternity.

As yet, we are full of ourselves with our minds, our ideas, our ambitions, our greed, our anger, our hard-nosed economics and our steely resolutions. There is very little space in this noise for a little golden note to come and play its little tune. It awaits its hour when man has had his fill of what he wants or what he thinks he wants. Perhaps, it waits for his cup to overflow, when there will be just a little space for the golden note to simply trickle in.

Every Moment, True and Free

L ife is like that…what are we to do? We must accept life as it is. Life has its own logic but our minds are unable to fathom it. Small bits and pieces we make sense of, but the larger part, or the whole, eludes us. Is this a jigsaw puzzle that we can solve with trial and error? Or is it an endless maze, defying solution? Whatever it is, we are faced with it.

Photo: Pradeep Malhotra

Is it a face-off between what we want and what life wants? Can a trade-off be done with some give and take? But what can we trade? How do we trade our life's desires with what life wants? Are our lives and 'life' two different things? And if they are, why would we be here? If they are not, we must know what life expects of us. Does life go by expectations? Or does it simply flow? It simply is. It lives in this moment. It delights in this moment. It is aware in this moment. It lies content in this moment. It does not examine the past or the future.

Is the 'now' what it is all about, the here and the now? Is it an ever present here and now, alert at each moment, a warm presence at each moment, an acceptance of all that is, that takes all in its embrace? Is it a moment that is all knowing, all revealing, an explosion of light, lighting all things, an instant vision, an instant revelation that unravels? Perhaps there are no secrets, no mysteries. There is only an opening of our eyes, of our minds, of channels that were blocked, of eyes that refused to see or could not see because the time was not right. We had yet to move from our evolutionary past, a slow progress, step by step. We were not ready for too great a light that would only have blinded us or sent us back.

Perhaps this light has appeared earlier too, but man was not ready then. But is man ready now, to take the next evolutionary step? Nature is ready and making her call. But is man willing? Is he prepared and able? There is a strange disquiet in the heart of man, but we know why. There is a strange yearning too, for we know not what. In an agonised blindness, man lurches from refuge to refuge, trying to find a safer harbour for his fragile ship which struggles and needs an anchor. The anchor too dissolves, for it is made of sand. So, where to now, he asks his soul. Where is my last haven, my last sanctuary, when all seems lost?

It lies within, says a revealing light. It always was within. It always was within your heart. It lies within the heart of every thing. It sings its song of delight in all things you see, in every moment, true and free.

Living Fully in the Moment

Anxiety, an existential anxiety, was the focus of our discussion the other evening, as my friend, Gurinder, and I took a walk in the park. We are confronted each moment with an existential anxiety that dissolves only in moments of self-forgetfulness, those moments when we are living fully in the moment.

Does being busy have anything to do with living in the moment? Can we be so busy that we have no time to think? Perhaps, this just might be evading the issue. The moment our 'busyness' is over, anxiety and doubt are back with a bang, perhaps a bigger bang. After conquering half the world, Alexander the Great was where he started. He felt unfulfilled and felt a great vacuum in his being. He realised when his time came that he would go empty handed. What would he carry with him—his 'emptiness,' his 'busyness'?

Look at people who have been busy all their lives; today, many do not know what to do. Time is a burden for them. What can they do to 'kill' time they ask? If we can kill time, will injury not be the result? An injury inflicted on the self.

Let us take each moment as it comes, unperturbed at the variety of situations it brings. Let us look forward to its surprises, the gifts that it brings, something new, something never seen or done the same way before, something never to happen the same way ever again, unique, once in a lifetime.

The Divine exists through us at this moment. We are its chosen instruments, nodes of its consciousness, vibrating to its frequency, sparks of an eternal fire that remembers! We must never cease to remember; our body's cells must now consciously remember, from moment to moment, that we are that eternal fire. This eternal fire takes all in its loving glow, consumes all in its golden hue, transforms all and brings each thing back to its divine source. I, my creator and all creation are one, indivisible.

Life takes a new turn and all illusions are shattered. Barriers, doubt and confusion give way to that which is whole, complete, and full of love and peace and unites our earthly existence with the life divine.

Man's Consciousness...Now Ready for a New Possibility

There is a cycle to the nature of events each day, each month, each year. Things move in cycles, in some fixed order. Time and space are inextricably linked to this cyclical movement. Evolution itself is a kind of cyclical progression, moving in ever-widening circles, taking all things in its sweep.

Is evolution a dumbing down or a flattening? Or is it a rising of all things to their true consciousness? Could it be that what we are seeing is a universalisation of consciousness? It is a rapid movement today, blindingly rapid. We need to keep pace with its momentum. We need to evolve just as nature wants us to. We must be nature's collaborators, comrades in arms. This consciousness is showing the path to unity.

Photo: Pradeep Malhotra

Every structure is interlinked, deeply intertwined… totally enmeshed with the other. We separate and break things at our peril. We need to see things as whole and complete. There is a deep underlying order to things, despite a superficial chaos or disorder. Is chaos, too, a hidden form of order? Could chaos be an order that is unrecognised? Look at particles in turbulent water. Observe these particles when the turbulence is removed. Could it be that our present turbulence is a harbinger of a wider order and harmony to follow?

Will the present disorder lead to a greater order? Does nature abhor disorder? Or does nature create disorder for a higher purpose? Nothing remains settled for long before disorder raises its head. Is anything that is settled for too long a kind of stagnancy, a kind of death? Does nature abhor decay and death? Or are decay and death just instruments for evolving a higher order, a higher consciousness? Is death just a temporary expedient, something transitional? Through death, man transits to another consciousness; each successive life and death is a successive progression in this consciousness.

Man has reached a terminal stage in his collective consciousness, a stage that must be surpassed, that has reached criticality. It is now pregnant with possibility. It can go either way. Man can annihilate himself and the planet or reach a new equilibrium where consciousness and physical evolution go hand-in-hand, in harmony and unsurpassed progression, where life takes on a totally new meaning. Is it perhaps the emergence of a fresh new dawn, where life and consciousness march in step with our destiny, a divine destiny envisioned in the womb of creation?

Moving Onto Another Voyage

It has been a night of cold, thunder and rain, followed by a day, dark with the promise of more thunder and rain. I want to be in a safe place, with a hot cup of coffee and a nice comforting book to hold and read. We all want to be in our own snug little worlds, far from the world of incessant change and care. What is it in us that does not for long let us be in peace, leading the secure and complete lives that we might wish to lead?

The world seems to be getting more complex with each passing day. It is more of everything…much, much more. Everything is being grossly amplified. Our lives, however, feel strangely diminished, as if the humanity and scale are being squeezed out. Are we being de-scaled? Re-scaled? Is something or someone telling us that we need to now grow into oversized boots? That our sights were set too low? That we are much bigger and vaster than we seem to be? Was it a big misunderstanding? We have not been able to understand who exactly we are. Is that the next step, to know who we really are and where we are going? If we know who we are, we may know where we must go.

So, we start with the first step. Who are we? Why are we here? Where are our origins? What is our inheritance? We go deep, deep down into the recess of human memory. We go into the recesses of our deepest intuitions, into our earliest recollections of a collective memory, into a search for our collective soul. We go into our deepest aspirations, into our deepest longings, into our very essence.

Our very essence is the spirit, presently materially embodied. It is part of the universal spirit, part of a creative principle. It is, in essence, divine and creative. It is fundamentally and wholly rooted in the divine and creative. It is part and parcel of a dynamic, evolving, creative consciousness. Its role on earth is to manifest this consciousness to perfection. It is a golden beam of light that wants to manifest. It is a beam that wants to shower gold in every direction. We are its instruments to manifest its shining riches.

We are in a state of self-forgetfulness at present. We have forgotten our divine origins. We are enmeshed in the material, the superficial; the topsoil conceals all that is hidden. We are like the iceberg, whose tip is visible; its vast body is well hidden below, submerged. The time has come for this hidden part of our being to re-emerge, to move onto another voyage, a voyage of consciousness.

Sparkling Once Again

The water lines in our area are choked. A fine mud oozes out as the plumber opens joints and taps hard on the water pipes. A thorough cleaning and unclogging is needed. A strange parallel is seen all over: roads and by-lanes are choked, schools and classrooms are choked, services and utilities are choked. Everywhere we look, things are choked; even our minds seem to be choked. It is too much of everything; we are crammed and saturated. All our lifelines are blocked by noise, pollution, environmental degradation, confusion and collapse of authority. The law of the jungle is at times no law at all.

Photo: Pradeep Malhotra

It is time for a cleansing, when everything is scrubbed clean and made sparkling again. All our preconceived ideas must be sent to the recycling bin. They have outlived their time. Their time is over and gone, yet they persist. They cling on desperately. The old world is an anchor they cannot relinquish. If they release the old, what is there to grasp and hold on to, they cry.

Our foundations are being rocked with a vengeance. Our philosophies and religions are being questioned. Everything is in a mix-up: the old and the new in a virtual *potpourri,* trans-global and intercontinental. We are floundering in quicksand and it is quick, sucking everything it sees into a whirlpool of unimaginable proportions, a virtual black hole.

But could this be another face of a virtual cleansing? Like a forest fire that destroys everything in its wake yet leaves the ground full of rich nutrients for a fresh new cycle, our individual and collective consciousness is now being shaken to the core and stir fried. Maybe the result will be a very tasty dish. At present, we have the feeling of being skewered and marinated simultaneously. We can feel the pain of all who are going through this evolutionary process. We are sensitive to the touch. Our wounds are raw; the world situation is a rubbing of salt into these wounds.

We feel the wounds and pain of every creature. In their salvation, lies our own. No man is an island, not anymore. For whom do these bells toll? For me, for you, for all of us! These bells herald a new life, a radical wrenching out of an old, obsolete long-gone past. They herald the brand new. The fresh, the new!

Catch me if you Can...

A sudden, passing glimpse provides the realisation that many planes of consciousness touch our beings at any given point of time but we are unaware. Living, waking, sleeping, dead, all is one continuum; we have given them different names.

Our lives, our bodies, are at the cutting edge of evolution but we are not aware. Nature and evolution are taking us to the next rung. We are to surpass all that has been so far. Mind, pain and desire were the goad and the movers, but now it is to be a conscious collaboration with the Divine. A co-evolution is in the air. We are co-players with the Divine, seeing through and participating in his *leela*, his unbridled creativity. We are no longer passive receptacles, we are co-creators. God is reaching out to man and now, man is reaching out to God. It is a divine moment!

Uncertain and full of clamour, our hearts are hesitant, full of fear, trepidation and anxiety. We are in a state of confusion; what is happening, we cry. Is this the hour to end all hours? All past certainties are at an end and we are bereft of our ancient moorings. Cultural and social structures are breaking down. Is it a free for all? Is it a victory of the strongest, the law of the jungle, where the only victor is fire and death? Is earth in its final throes, only awaiting its last moments? Or is it the hour of the unexpected, when earth takes a radical turn, whole and complete? Have we come to the end of a materialist culture, has a *yuga* ended? Or is a new age and consciousness being heralded?

All the signs are there. All of mankind is in rebellion mode today and a revolution is in the air. We no longer want the old ways of looking at and doing things; all that is past. The old ways no longer work, nor can we put old wine in new bottles. We are heady with a new wine made of diviner stuff. Its portents glimmer in the smallest thing we see. They laugh and skip with us when we are at our intuitive best. They disappear without a trace, leaving a taste of dust, when we are unaware, when we lose track of our spontaneity and consciousness of the moment.

It is a game of hide-and-seek we play with the Divine. It hides and we seek. We hide and it seeks. It hides itself in all, even that little floating speck in the air, in that beam of light, in the cry of a child, in the twilit sky. It cries, 'come and seek me if you can'. And when we do, it hides again, a consciousness ever at play. Now I am, now I am not, catch me if you can! I run to catch. I put you deep in my heart so that you can never escape again. This time, you are safely locked in my very being itself and I have thrown away the key!

The Quest for the Golden Key

We are closer to one another than we can ever imagine. Distance has no meaning. A heart beating on the moon is just as close. It is a throbbing of heartbeats all the way, throbbing to an eternal tune. The same consciousness touches each heart, each accompanying the other.

There is a symphony, with the Divine as conductor; all we need to do is to play our parts. One wrong note and the symphony out of sync. But the conductor gives us many an opportunity, chance after chance. He wants us to get it perfect. We must be in it together. Can we imagine a symphony with the pianist or the chief trombonist missing? Each has a unique role to play, one that no one else can play.

Photo: Pradeep Malhotra

The world and each person in it are placed in a unique position. This present world and this present moment are unique. Such a combination has never existed before nor will it ever exist again. What happens in the future depends on how we play our parts today, at this very moment. The eternal watches to see how we play our parts, for in what we do now lies future evolution.

To know the divine plan, we need to go deep within. All answers lie within, hidden in the depths of our hearts. The golden key is hidden there. God wanted us to explore many continents before we came to the quest for the golden key. And now, the time has come. We have explored many continents, other worlds, planets and yet the search has been elusive.

The perfect answer lies within, safely hidden in the silence of our hearts. It has remained hidden for aeons, for centuries, with a purpose. We were not ready to see the truth, to face the truth. Its light was too great for our human eyes. Our eyes needed to be shielded or they would go blind. Bit by bit, the shield could come down, would come down. Our inner eye has been preparing over centuries. Today, we sense that a time might be approaching for a revelation. The Divine is now revealing itself to its children. 'Come, let us play,' the Divine seems to say. 'No more hide-and-seek,' we say. We have been seeking and you have been hiding all along, dear God. 'My children, I have been seeking you all along and it is you who have been hiding.'

It has been a comedy of errors, dear God. We could never imagine that we were the ones sought. We had hidden our faces from you and we sought refuge in everything but you. We open our eyes today with a prayer on our lips: 'let your sunshine bring to us the life divine with each passing moment'. *'Chokher aloy dekhechilem chokher bahire...'* as Rabindranath Tagore invoked and sang.

Unblock that Block

Block! Block! Block! Is life a series of blocking and unblocking at every step, at every stage? Today, it is a blocked career, tomorrow a blocked relationship or a blocked talent, a blocked road…just more blocks at every step.

The block should be recognised for what it is—just a block. It is not something permanent; it can be dismantled. Just as a road that is blocked clears up as soon as the object causing the block is moved, we must remove the blocks we have placed in our minds, of prejudice, bias, preference, hatred, desire, likes and dislikes. There are other blocks: the fear of the new and untried, the strange and the nation next door.

No, I won't do this. No, I can't do that. No, this is impossible. Why is this red? It should be black. The mind is fixated on something and that becomes a block. Habit too is a block. Just because we have always done something in a certain way, must it be done the same way yet again?

Travel is a great eye-opener. It helps unblock our minds. New people, new situations and new ways of seeing and doing things. The stranger helps us unblock our deepest prejudices. We see him and things in new light. We unblock and reach out to a new part of ourselves which we did not know existed. We are brand new in many parts, so brand new that the packaging has yet to be opened. It is a gift we give ourselves, a gift of fresh new eyes at every moment. It is as if the Divine has created the world just this moment, oven-fresh, with the aroma still lingering. We are brand new. We are the new man, the new woman, the new child, on a new road, with a new song. It is a new story.

This moment is always new, untouched by the past or the future. Can we live from moment to moment in this ever-bubbling freshness? One whiff and we are recharged. Everything is once again fresh and original; there is nothing duplicate or stale about it. Everything is unblocked!

Today, the country is blocked. Nothing is moving. What is the way out? Can we stand back a bit? Can we be silent? Can we just observe? Can we just let things be for a bit? Can we stop pulling and pushing? Can we just listen to each other? Can we give space to the other? Can we let a million flowers bloom? There are many ways of looking at things, many ways of doing things. Let us not block ourselves.

Just as air and water remain fresh only when they move, so must we. Everything is relative. Everything changes when even a single dimension is altered. When we bring in the dimension of silence into our lives, we touch other dimensions too. 'In peace and silence the eternal manifests… allow nothing to disturb you and the eternal will manifest.' It is in silence that the divine grace helps smooth life's blocked paths.

The Glow of a Lamp

The glow of a lamp in a temple, the glow of a flame in the temple of our hearts…may this glow remain till our last breath. It is this glow that carries us through the many ups and downs of life. It is part of an eternal light that leads us through darkness, obstacles and pitfalls, back to where we truly belong.

I carry this light, my original home, with me, no matter where I am. I carry it in my heart. I carry it in my being. I carry it waking and sleeping. I carry it when I think, when I act and when I do. I carry it in the very essence of my being.

Photo: Pradeep Malhotra

My light, my home and I are one. My creator and I are one. My origins and my wanderings are one. All trails lead to the One, no matter where I might begin. Perhaps, the trail and destination are one. Perhaps, existence itself is a destination, ever fluid, ever evolving. We arrive at every stage. Arrival and departure are one.

We are not abandoned. We are not lost. We are forever safe and loved in the eternal's heart. The eternal has but leased us to the movement of time for the fulfilment of a creation it holds dear. We are its playmates. We have taken on roles to do its bidding, to manifest its splendour.

The divine splendour must manifest in every nook, in every dark space, on earth, on seas, hills, mountains and in wide spaces. Its splendour must manifest in galaxies, in all creation. The sound of its name must ring in the temple of every heart, its vibrations reaching out to eternity. The billowing mists of its presence spread deep into the hunger of my soul, making me one with its command. Its message lies in every flicker of flame, the early beginnings of an ever-growing blaze. Wave upon wave of a holy fire, a purging and resurgence, a constant widening of consciousness.

A love that is distilled pure, drop by drop. Nectar so pure it intoxicates. We find God's hand in every touch. Everything is a vibration of the divine command. All colours and hues are one, refractions of a greater light imbued with a power to delight, to create, to rejuvenate. Creation brought to the threshold of another wave is a promise of heaven on earth long made. A promise made by God to himself coming true today.

Where is the Buddha Point?

The middle path is one of balance, a way the Buddha has shown. It is the way to harmony and a gateway to bliss. Torn between extremes, the mind longs for an inner balance and harmony, in the face of conflicting demands and situations. We go in one direction first and then in another, but the result is always the same—the mind remains restless, dissatisfied. The further we move towards one pole, the greater the siren cry of the other. We are caught in an oscillation, relentless at times. Is this to be our fate for the remainder of our lives?

The Buddha too went through this dilemma many centuries ago. He went through the extremes of emotion and suffering. He went through the motions of debating and rejecting one solution after another. He rejected the demands of his own body. He let himself be inflicted with sufferings to see if there was an answer in these. He had rejected wealth, power and pleasures, which were his by right. He went to the very end of extremes and yet his mind found no solace.

And then, one day, in his deeply silent meditations, an answer came.

The answer lay not in extremes, in pleasures or in suffering, but in a third position which neither desired nor rejected things. All things are part of our reality, our human experience. All things are part of our evolution and consciousness. Each must be experienced, but we need not be attached to the experience or reject it. We accept 'what is' in our stride. We see the scales in their weighing motion, going up and down, oscillating endlessly till they reach some golden equilibrium. Is this the point where man's mind should be centred? A golden equilibrium where all stands still, all conflicts are resolved and all dualities are made one? Where man and the Divine are one? Is this the point where the Buddha attained *nirvana*? Is this the point where he saw a breakthrough for mankind? Is this the Buddha point for each of us?

Can we bring our ever-fluctuating lives to a golden mean? By contemplating the golden mean in all things, by imbibing its essence in our lives, by living it from moment to moment, by becoming one with it. We accept nothing, we reject nothing; we see things as they are. Things are what they are. The tiger is a tiger. The earth's rotation is what it is. We witness all things and are not perturbed. Our hearts and minds are centred in the middle path, in balance; in harmony with our eternal witness self.

Man, the Envoy of the Divine

The phone rings intermittently, early in the morning, with so many agendas. Family, friends and colleagues want to rope you into this, that or the other. We wonder how we can retain our sanity with so many demands. We need to be in some neutral mode—be in this world, but not of it. The world's needs and rush will continue no matter what. Can I restrict myself to what I can do and at my own pace instead of breaking my head over it? I must learn to say no. A positive 'no' saves us from many an unwanted situation. Listen to all with respect but listen to your own heart's counsel.

Photo: Pradeep Malhotra

In this age of incessant clamour, the voice of our heart and soul is drowned in the din. We must slow down and be peaceful. In silence, we can hear the soul speak, through intuition, through acts of love, through spontaneity. Let this spark of love rise like fragrant incense smoke. Let it permeate every pore of your being.

Let each be what each essentially is. Let us remove all the layers we have superimposed on ourselves, of our wants, desires and preferences. We should peel them off one by one, even as the next one makes its presence felt. Perhaps, we need a yoga to bring us back to our essence, to a circle completing itself.

Has humanity come to the end of a circle? This chaos and confusion is a symbol and a sign. A new energy and vibration are in the air, a vibration that has caught mankind unawares. Man is still deeply rooted in his past. He finds this new energy unsettling, but at the same time, is deeply attracted to its vibrations. He must release something to get something. But what is it that he must release and what will he get in return?

He may need to release his fears, his desires, his need to dominate and his deep-seated insecurities. He is in a state of self-forgetfulness. He has forgotten that his origins are divine. He is an envoy of the divine, a helper to the cause of bringing a new consciousness into the earth's atmosphere. Each thing is to be made divine, even the most material. It is a superhuman task, and we have asked for it to be given to us—to make this earth as it is in heaven.

We must start with ourselves. All change must start with oneself. The repercussions of one small change are enormous. One thing touches another and its waves are felt far and wide. The ripples of a new consciousness are in the air. We must catch them with our nets flung wide.

The End...or a Very New Beginning?

As I put on the CD, the sounds come softly rolling in. I hum to the tune of 'Ave Maria,' which is soothing beyond measure. There is something about this music that is so uplifting, so inspiring. Just yesterday, we saw a film on the life of Begum Akhtar, a woman with a mind so much her own, inspired, whimsical, demanding and with romance in her soul that resonated harmoniously even to pain. Both love and pain took on a new meaning.

They don't make people like her anymore. What has changed? Is it our perceptions of ourselves and the world too, perhaps? We have taken ourselves too much for granted. We have taken our place in creation for granted. But all is now changing before our very startled eyes. Who or what are we, is the question staring us in the face today. Who am I? What is this body? What is this collection of memories, this bunch of assorted desires in conflict with each other?

Where do I go from here? This vantage point is my summit today, the summit of all my aspirations and desires. From this summit, what do I see? Although I have moved, I have not really moved very much. My desires remain, although they may have changed shape. The old actors around me have moved on and a new set of characters are my comrades. But then, something else has changed too!

I feel a change in my consciousness. I am more aware of things than I was ever before. What were nascent bubbles then have now exploded, metamorphosed into shapes vaguely recognisable. Everything has evolved as has my consciousness. A co-evolution has taken place very quietly, stealthily. It has moved all things to where they were meant to be. It has brought to nought many things we thought were permanent, imperishable. In the march of consciousness, nothing is permanent except its own progression. All things must become co-equal in consciousness and move on. Every thing must become conscious, fully conscious. Everything must wake up to its essential truth.

Today, our earth is becoming conscious. We are bidding goodbye to our old selves, bringing in something brand new, something never seen before. Is man in the process of reinventing himself without even being aware? All the signs are there. Someone or something has heard man's deepest call, felt his deepest longings. Someone or something is responding to this call. The air is full of a message, but the signs clash with clamour around. We are confused. Is this the end…or a very new beginning?

Let us silence our hearts and our minds in good measure to receive this blessing of blessings. Could this be the hour of the unexpected, the incalculable, and the immeasurable? Could this be the hour of God…an hour when when all things become possible?